Like a Woman in Travail

Like a Woman in Travail

—— Human Suffering in Biblical Perspective ——

John A. Porter

WIPF & STOCK · Eugene, Oregon

LIKE A WOMAN IN TRAVAIL
Human Suffering in Biblical Perspective

Copyright © 2024 John A. Porter. All rights reserved. Except for brief quotations in critical publications or reviews, no part of this book may be reproduced in any manner without prior written permission from the publisher. Write: Permissions, Wipf and Stock Publishers, 199 W. 8th Ave., Suite 3, Eugene, OR 97401.

Wipf & Stock
An Imprint of Wipf and Stock Publishers
199 W. 8th Ave., Suite 3
Eugene, OR 97401

www.wipfandstock.com

PAPERBACK ISBN: 979-8-3852-0706-0
HARDCOVER ISBN: 979-8-3852-0707-7
EBOOK ISBN: 979-8-3852-0708-4

VERSION NUMBER 01/22/24

Scripture quotations are from The Holy Bible, English Standard Version (ESV), copyright © 2001 by Crossway. Used by permission. All rights reserved.

Excerpts from Eric Doyle OFM, *Bringing Forth Christ: Five Feasts of the Child Jesus by St Bonaventure*, Fairacres Publications 90 (Oxford: SLG Press, ©1984) are reproduced by kind permission of the Convent of the Incarnation, Oxford, England.

For D. H. Clark and A. R. Knapp

Pangs have seized me, like the pangs of a woman in travail.
　　　　　—Isaiah 21:3

Contents

Prologue | ix
Acknowledgements | xv

Introduction: Suffering As Birth Pangs | 1

Chapter 1: The Birth Pangs of Israel | 18

Chapter 2: The Birth Pangs of Jesus | 33

Chapter 3: The Birth Pangs of the Church | 47

Chapter 4: The Birth Pangs of the Christian | 60

Chapter 5: The Birth Pangs of the Cosmos | 73

Epilogue | 91
Appendix 1: The Bones of Joseph: A Case Study in Bringing Forth Christ | 93
Appendix 2: Bringing Forth Christ as *Imitatio Mariae* | 113
Appendix 3: From *Bringing Forth Christ: Five Feasts of the Child Jesus by St. Bonaventure* | 119
Bibliography | 125
Scripture Index | 129

Prologue

> Trembling took hold of them there, anguish as of a woman in labor. *Psalm 48:6*

THE PHILOSOPHER FRIEDRICH NIETZSCHE once wrote that "what really arouses indignation against suffering is not suffering itself but the senselessness of suffering." Humanity's "problem," he went on, "is not suffering itself, but that there [is] no answer to the crying question, 'Why do I suffer?'. . . Man, the bravest of animals and the one most accustomed to suffering, does not repudiate suffering as such: he desires it, he even seeks it out, provided he is shown a meaning for it, a purpose of suffering. The meaninglessness of suffering, not suffering itself, was the curse that lay over mankind."[1] Indeed, if we believe that the pain in our lives is random and pointless, we are ill-equipped to bear it with equanimity, but are, rather, inclined to throw up our hands and abandon ourselves to dejection and despair. "Why (here some will interject, "in God's name") must we be subjected to this misery?" Even such a devout Christian as the lay theologian C. S. Lewis, writing about his sense of loss over the death of his wife after a long and painful illness, asked rhetorically if "all these notes [aren't] the senseless writhings of a man who won't accept the fact that there is nothing we can do with suffering except to suffer it."[2]

---

1. Kaufmann, *Basic Writings of Nietzsche*, 504.
2. Lewis, *Grief Observed*, 29.

PROLOGUE

As Nietzsche asserts and Lewis demonstrates, what we must have, above all, is a purpose for our pain. It's not enough to believe, as Christians do—at least on a theoretical level—that it has come upon us, collectively, as the result of our disobedience, which originally enjoined hardship upon us and continues to work us woe. We stand in need of a rationale that will render the painfulness of life intelligible and therefore endurable in this world—a purpose to believe in, and one which will be vindicated in the world to come.

Such a purpose is boldly set forth from the outset in the Bible, and reinforced constantly throughout its pages. It may be simply and succinctly stated this way: suffering is but the pangs of birth. It is not pain that comes and goes (or comes and stays) for no discernible reason. On the contrary, it is, of its very nature, the herald of an outcome—an end, a result—which is none other than life from the womb into which the tomb has been converted by Jesus's death and resurrection. The pain we must endure is endurable, therefore, not because it ultimately leads to death and an end of our misery (as it most certainly does in this life), but precisely because it is the inalienable accompaniment of the divinely-ordained path by which we eventually enter into "that which is truly life" (1 Tim 6:19).

In the main, and with good reason, those who write about suffering do so in order to address the questions which its existence inevitably raises.[3] Why do the righteous suffer? Does God cause suffering? Do we suffer because of our sins? Where is God in our suffering? How can we reconcile suffering with God's goodness? For the most part, all seem to agree that, while the existence of suffering itself may remain forever a mystery, its usefulness is justified in a variety of ways: to make us stronger, to teach us humility, to create in us empathy for others, and so on.

Treatments of the subject from a Christian perspective tend to focus largely on attempts to reconcile the power and goodness of God with the pervasiveness of pain in his creation, and then to move on to his reasons for permitting his creatures to suffer. These typically make use of the metaphors of the furnace[4] (Isa 48:10) and the forge or the fire (1 Pet 1:6–7) for refining personal faith. More general approaches follow in the venerable

---

3. Some years ago a best-seller appeared that captured the essence of this approach in its title: "When Bad Things Happen to Good People."

4. A good example is Timothy Keller's *Walking with God through Pain and Suffering* (2013), the three main parts of which are headed "Understanding the Furnace," "Facing the Furnace," and "Walking with God in the Furnace."

tradition of attempting to "justify the ways of God to man,"[5] known by the technical term "theodicy." Richard Rice's *Suffering and the Search for Meaning: Contemporary Responses to the Problem of Pain* (2014) is representative. After beginning with a chapter entitled "My God, Why?" (subtitled "The Question That Never Goes Away"), Rice proceeds to chapters with subtitles like ""Perfect Plan Theodicy," "Soul Making Theodicy," "Cosmic Conflict Theodicy," "Openness of God Theodicy," "Finite God Theodicy," "Protest Theodicies," and concludes with "Fragments of Meaning." The mystery of suffering thus becomes more of a philosophical problem to be illuminated than a theological challenge to be met. All the while, suffering itself is stoically accepted under the limitations of our knowledge and understanding of God's largely inscrutable workings.

But what if the secret to the enigma of suffering, far from being shrouded in impenetrable darkness, is transparently set forth in the very beginning, where it is embodied in God's immediate response to human sin, and from where it is progressively unfolded as the inner dynamic of so-called "salvation history"? What if the mystery of suffering is not its meaning or purpose in an abstract sense, but its regenerative power, which constitutes its true quality and character? What if suffering, in its essence, is a form of precisely those birth pangs through which a new creation, enucleated in the risen Christ, is being brought into existence to replace the old, corrupted as it is by the sin which occasioned the suffering in the first place?

Such is the thesis of this book. It does not set out either to formulate a theodicy or to provide pastoral guidance—though some of both may be found incidentally in its pages—but primarily to discern and articulate the fundamental framework found in Scripture for understanding the existence, meaning, and purpose of suffering in the divine plan for humanity. Our claim, in short, is that suffering itself demands to be seen as nothing less than the means by which God both fully reveals himself and finally redeems his fallen creation.

The reader will have noticed that this book's subtitle is "Human Suffering in Biblical Perspective." The Bible, no doubt, offers many perspectives on suffering in God's world, but our contention in these pages is that the primary metaphor through which we are invited to view it is that of birth pangs, pain that is directed—like the rays of light through a prism—to the focal point of the bringing forth of Jesus Christ in glory as the redeemer and savior of all who put their trust in him. This invitation being accepted, we are

---

5. John Milton, *Paradise Lost*.

enabled, moreover, better to see the fullness of birth pangs' unique significance, derived as it is partly from their association with the growth, development, and emergence of new life; partly from their promise of a longed-for and auspicious outcome; and partly from their transitory nature.

The underlying perspective of the Scriptures on suffering, then, is not so much something that they teach as something that they embody. Its inner dynamic is the Incarnation. If the whole purpose of suffering is the bringing forth of the redeemer, and if that means God-becoming-man, then, given the realities of human propagation, humanity must first suffer as a woman does in labor in order for that to be accomplished. If there is any such thing as a "theology of suffering" in the Bible, then, it is found in the metaphor of the pain associated with bringing a child into the world. This fact becomes apparent to anyone who follows the long arc of the biblical narrative, but it has rarely, if ever, received the prominence it deserves.

The motif of birth pangs pervades the Scriptures, beginning with their imposition in the third chapter of Genesis and continuing to the vision of the woman in travail in the twelfth chapter of the book of Revelation. It reaches its apex in the Passion of our Lord, recounted in all four Gospels, when Jesus "labors," on the one hand, to be "born" through death and resurrection, and on the other, to bring forth the Church from his side in the form of water and blood, representing the sacraments of Baptism and Eucharist.

The Old Testament provides the necessary background for this, equating the sufferings of God's people, Israel, to a woman crying out in her labor, and in turn relating this to what becomes known through the apocalyptic writers of the inter-testamental period as the "messianic woes": the tribulation that necessarily accompanies the coming forth of the promised king and savior.

For its part, the New Testament employs the imagery of childbirth to depict what St. Peter describes in his first sermon as a kind of "conversion" of the tomb into a womb by the resurrection of Jesus. It is then applied to the birth of the Church and the transformation of the Christian by a twofold development. First, there is the "gestation," as it were, of the Church/Christian within Jesus, preliminary to the manifestation of both together in Jesus's image at his return in glory. Simultaneous to this is the complementary gestation of Jesus within the Church/Christian preliminary to his manifestation in their life and in the world. In an extension of this imagery,

PROLOGUE

at the final consummation the whole cosmos will be released from its labor in a rebirth that constitutes its renewal.

We begin, in the introduction, with the adaptation of human propagation to a new end both before and after humankind's Fall, and the new role subsequently assigned to suffering. In chapter 1, we examine the vocation of Israel, epitomized in the Virgin Mary, to bring forth the promised Messiah. Chapter 2 sets out two complementary views of the Passion of Jesus as pangs of birth—both his own "birth" through resurrection, and subsequently, that of the Church. The following two chapters elucidate the birth pangs entailed in the reciprocal indwelling of Christ and his Church (chapter 3), and of Christ and the Christian (chapter 4). The fifth and final chapter shows how these birth pangs come to their climax in the bringing forth of "new heavens and a new earth in which righteousness dwells" (2 Pet 3:13).

To those who may think it audacious or presumptuous for a man—that is, a male human being—to undertake to write about something he cannot, in the nature of things, experience firsthand for himself, I plead the precedent of men like Isaiah and Jeremiah who were audacious enough to liken their own pain, and the pain of their compatriots, to that of a woman in travail (Isa 21:3; Jer 6:24). "Can a man bear a child?" asks Jeremiah rhetorically, and then seems to answer his own question in the affirmative: "Why then do I see every man with his hands on his stomach like a woman in labor?" (Jer 30:6).

Being, however, neither a prophet nor divinely inspired (nor, for that matter—as my wife and children will readily attest—an exemplary sufferer), I claim only that being human is in itself sufficient minimum qualification for the task. Case in point: as I prepare this book for the press, I am convalescing from abdominal surgery and have often found myself literally placing my hands on my stomach in a vain attempt somehow to make the pain stop. While the degree of my suffering is in no way comparable to the agony of maternal labor, I am nonetheless reminded daily of the need faced by women in childbirth to work through their pangs for the sake of a hoped-for and joyfully-anticipated outcome unimaginably greater than mere cessation.

Feast of the Nativity John A. Porter
December 25, 2023
Pittsburgh, PA

Acknowledgements

THIS BOOK IS THE long-gestated fruit of an invitation offered me "out of the blue" one autumn day in 1983 by my friend Dan Clark in a cubicle that we shared as teaching fellows in a graduate writing program at the University of Pittsburgh. It was an invitation—like the one Andrew extended to his brother Peter (John 1:40–42) and that Philip gave to his neighbor Nathanael (John 1:45)—to "come and see" Jesus (John 1:46). Given the trajectory of my life at that point, I am quite sure that had anyone but he asked, I would have declined. How glad I am that he did . . . and I did not! Sure enough, going together, we encountered Jesus himself in the preaching of Rick Knapp, for whose faithfulness in proclaiming the finished work of Christ I will ever be grateful, and under whose tutelage I first felt what I can only describe as the inward "quickening" of the theme that has never ceased to enthrall me: Jesus's conversion—by his death and resurrection—of the tomb into a womb for all who believe in him and are baptized in the name of the Father, and of the Son, and of the Holy Spirit.

I remain in the debt, as well, of all those others who have nurtured me on the journey, helping me in various ways to see more clearly that all our sufferings are indeed but the birth pangs of new life in Christ: the late Renwick Wright, who instilled in me an abiding love for the language and teaching of the New Testament; Steve Stratos, who modeled for me the care of a shepherd for his flock; Paul Copeland, who mentored me and wisely directed me away from academia and into pastoral ministry; the late Doug McGlynn, who first welcomed me on "the road to Canterbury" and then shepherded me through the ordination process to the priesthood; Fred Robinson, who somehow saw the makings of a catholic Christian in me and called me to be his curate; and the faithful people of Grace Anglican Church, in Pittsburgh, Pennsylvania, who chose me to be their pastor and walked alongside me as followers of Jesus.

My deepest gratitude goes also to my wife Beth, who lent her perspective as a mother and a physician on these musings, and without whose love, support, and encouragement I am quite sure these pages would never have seen the light of day.

Introduction

Suffering as Birth Pangs

> I will surely multiply your pain in childbearing; in pain you shall bring forth children. *Genesis 3:15*

IN THE VAST MAJORITY of non-mammalian animals, the propagation of offspring is—as far as we can tell—a painless process. Among insects, birds, fish, and reptiles, the female of the species bears its young by laying or depositing eggs with no discernible discomfort. The case is, however, markedly different for those species whose females reproduce by means of live birth. Indeed, only in the higher forms of life do "creatures cause pain by being born," as C. S. Lewis once said.[1]

And yet even here there are wide variances on the pain spectrum, judging by the relative length and intensity of the struggle involved in the expulsion of the offspring from its mother's body. Dolphins, on the one hand, appear to give birth without undue pain or struggle. On the other hand, primates as a whole undeniably experience parturition as a traumatic event. For none of our cousins, however—except in the most complicated cases—is the birthing process as extended in time or as intense in sensation as is the case for a human mother. We might expect that there would be a back story to this, and there is—in fact, a rather involved one.

---

1. Lewis, *Problem of Pain*, 14.

The Womb's Place

The womb undoubtedly had a special place in the evolutionary development of humanity according to the creative purposes of God. This was surely due to his foresight of its role in the incarnation of his Son as the man Jesus, who would, in time, be conceived in the womb of the blessed Virgin. When, therefore, we attempt to locate more precisely that impossible-to-determine time when the creator made man in his image (Gen 1:26–27) from the dust of the earth (Gen 2:5–7), and brought forth the woman from his side to be his mate (Gen 2:21–23), we do well—for reasons that will appear shortly—to look for the emergence of the womb in its accustomed orientation within the woman's body.[2]

According to the widely-accepted tenets of evolutionary science, humans ultimately emerged from a process that began with lower life forms. The means of propagation developed along with this process, and was, of course, the "mechanism" by which the process itself was carried on. Differentiation of male and female played an intrinsic part, the two sexes developing complementary genitalia, which included, in the case of the female, an inward receptacle—the uterus, or womb—for the deposit of the male sperm. Here, following the sperm's fertilization of the female ovum, the subsequent growth of a new organism to propagate the species by means of live birth was enabled to take place.

Given anatomical limitations, we may safely surmise that there was never a time when the period of gestation within the female body did not involve discomfort for the mother. The subsequent emergence of the fully-developed fetus with its large head through a relatively narrow birth canal in the pelvis likewise inevitably compounded this reality. Thus a measure of pain was the natural concomitant of childbirth for the woman, as it is for the female of every species propagating itself by giving birth to its young alive.

Not only does divine revelation not contradict this account (the "what" of the inner dynamic of evolutionary science), it allows room for the "how," and—even more crucially—supplements it with the all-important "why." On the evolution of the species, according to the teaching of the Church,

---

2. In what follows, we acknowledge the divergent but complementary explanations offered by science and by divine revelation, respectively, and at the same time we affirm our Christian commitment to a holistic understanding of God's creative work—that is, to the conviction that the "how" and "why" of the act of creation can be accommodated to the "what."

revelation superimposes what has fittingly been called an "involution,"³ a divine intervention at a point somewhere along the evolutionary continuum. This involution oriented the whole natural, physical process—from the beginning under God's creative control and direction—more fully and specifically to the fulfillment of his purpose for emerging humankind.

In catholic theology, such an involution is described in terms of a bestowal of a *donum supernaturale* (supernatural gift) on the male and the female. This is the counterpart, on the one hand, of their creation "in [God's] image" (Gen 1:26), and corresponds, on the other, to God's breathing into the man's nostrils of the "breath of life" (Gen 2:7). Prior to this intervention by God, as the Church broadly teaches, the species followed its natural evolutionary development unimpeded. Among other things, humans reproduced in the same way as other primates: notably, males copulating with females from a posterior position. Then, over a period of millennia, an evolutionary change took place that bears evidence of the postulated divine involution. The human species gradually assumed an upright walking position, unique among its cousins, and became *homo erectus.*

Coincident with this new development was another momentous physiological change. Female genitalia gradually adapted to uprightness of stature by migrating to a forward position between the legs, so that sexual intercourse between the male and the female became not only possible but also most natural in a face-to-face orientation. The way was thereby opened for their physical union to be not just a matter of biological necessity for the propagation of the species, but also a personal act expressive of the desire—gradually, we may posit, growing into affection and even love—that drew and bound them together. The state that eventually came about as a result is characterized by what the writer of the human creation account describes when he says: "Therefore a man shall leave his father and his mother and hold fast to his wife, and they shall become one flesh" (Gen 2:24).

This provides the context for the account of creation given in the first chapter of Genesis,⁴ which speaks of the making of "male and female" "in [God's] image" (Gen 1:27). What had been achieved in evolutionary terms was the potential for the man and the woman to be in conformity (admittedly as but a faint reflection) to an infinitely higher order of being.

---

3. For this term we are indebted to Francis J. Hall, who employs it in *Creation and Man*, volume 5 of his *Dogmatic Theology*, where he explains it as a form of "higher causation" and defines it as "divine in-breathing" (176).

4. It is generally agreed that this first account (Gen 1:26–30) is a later development than the second (Gen 2:5–23).

In short, they entered into a similar personal relation as the one that obtains between the Father and the Son, in which the Son is said to be both "at the Father's side" (*eis ton kolpon tou Patros*,[5] John 1:18)—as the woman, the man's "helper" (Gen 2:18) is to her mate—and, even more pointedly, "toward [*pros*] God" (John 1:1), or "face to face" with him. Only, therefore, when the love between the first and second Persons of the Godhead that this new orientation represents came also to characterize the union of the man and the woman in service of procreation could it be said that they—"male and female" together—were created in God's image,[6] since "God is love" (1 John 4:8).

Thus was the love interior to the Godhead replicated in the coming together of the creatures thereby made in the divine image. Birth pangs themselves, then, insofar as they were the consequence of the physical union of the man and woman for the propagation of the species, were initiated by love—the love that God both has (John 3:16) and is (1 John 4:8). This love became the source of the human act that unites the man and the woman, reproducing the divine image in their offspring as a result. In light of this, it is noteworthy, indeed, that human intercourse—in divine intention, at least, the quintessential act of love between a man and a woman—is euphemistically referred to as "making love."

In the scholastic terms of the Middle Ages, the involution of which we have spoken was called the *donum superadditum* (super-added gift), that is, a divine gift superimposed, as it were, on the evolutionary scheme. This was necessary, according to catholic theology, in order to fit and equip humankind, thereby made in God's image, for the divine vocation of sharing God's likeness (Gen 1:26), or actually becoming "like God" (Gen 3:5),[7] both in stewardship as God's vice-regent in the natural world of which humanity was a part, and in capacity for friendship and fellowship with God himself.

Whereas in its merely natural state mankind was, like other creatures, subject to death and bodily dissolution, the supernatural state to which the man and the woman were raised by God's intervention bestowed on them a conditional immortality. In other words, if they cooperated with

---

5. Traditionally translated "in the bosom of the Father."

6. The divine image in man is often associated with faculties such as knowledge, reason, will, and memory, but, as Gregory Dix observes, while these may be the "power" of the image, the image itself "lies rather in man's power of loving" (Dix, *Image and Likeness*, 22).

7. The temptation presented by the serpent to the woman was in the form of a shortcut to an outcome desired by God himself.

the grace given to them, they were (with God's assistance) capable of evading death and being spared the suffering that characterizes a mortal existence. Of special interest to us in this connection, this means that the woman was thereby relieved of the necessity of undergoing the pangs that naturally accompanied pregnancy and childbirth, or, at the very least, that she was given a generous reprieve—a kind of "divine epidural," if you will—from their otherwise onerous burden.

Alas, the disobedience of the man and the woman abrogated these arrangements. It caused God to withdraw his supernatural gift and return humanity, as it were, to its natural state. Now, not only was the *donum supernaturale* forfeited and the divine image therefore also defaced, but the divine likeness—in its incipient form—was lost. This consequence was communicated to the first man and woman in the form of "curses" imposed as a result of the Fall.[8]

The consequence for the woman was stated first, but—for good reason—only after God addressed the serpent that deceived her. As a matter of fact, the curse pronounced on the serpent served the purpose of declaring the new end to which the propagation of the human species would thereafter be directed. God said to the serpent, "I will put enmity between you and the woman, between your offspring and her offspring; he shall bruise your head, and you shall bruise his heel" (Gen 3:15).

Here we must pause briefly to clarify the significance of the word "offspring" as used in this passage, referring specifically to the progeny of the woman. The Hebrew term so translated is *zera*, which has a collective sense, that is, it refers to descendants as a whole rather than to a particular descendant. In its original context, therefore, the meaning appears to be that humanity in general will triumph over its adversary, rather than that any single person will gain the victory. From the perspective of the New Testament, however, this meaning has been expanded by several developments for which divine inspiration can be claimed.

The first development is that, in the Septuagint, the authorized Greek translation of the Old Testament, the pronoun referring to offspring—a

---

8. We must bear in mind that the account of the divine curses is a literary product of a relatively late period (probably between 800 and 500 BCE) and that it represents an interpretation of the original consequences of human transgression of the divine command. Those men responsible for it are reflecting on traditions handed down to them concerning the origins of sin and suffering in light of their experience of those two realities in their own day, and are expressing through it, by divine inspiration, their hope and expectation of ultimate deliverance and vindication.

Greek word (*sperma*) neuter in gender, like its Hebrew counterpart—is masculine: "he [*autos*] shall bruise your head." This is evidence of an ancient understanding that the offspring was, in fact, a male individual rather than a collective entity. Second, and even more importantly, St. Paul, writing under the inspiration of the Holy Spirit, while commenting on the promise of offspring to Abraham (Gen 12:7; 15:5), makes the argument—possible only because *sperma* also has a plural form, *spermata*—that the use of the singular form necessitates a reference not to "many" but to "one." Moreover, he explicitly identifies that "one" as "Christ" (Gal 3:16).

If what St. Paul asserts may be said to be true of Abraham's offspring, it is necessarily true of Eve's as well, since the descendants of Adam and Eve are traced through Abraham (Luke 3:23–36). In the end (this is the third development), since all redeemed humanity is said to be "in Christ" (Eph 1:3–14), the collective sense of offspring is ultimately included in the individual sense, applied as it is to Jesus. Thus, Satan's being crushed under the feet (Rom 16:20) of the Church, the "body" of Christ, is only the ultimate outworking of his head being bruised by Jesus, the "head" of the Church, through his death on the cross.

Returning now to the divine promise regarding the offspring of the woman, we find that it is the first allusion to descendants in this second creation account in Genesis. While the account in the first chapter of Genesis speaks in general terms of the man and the woman being fruitful, and multiplying and filling the earth (Gen 1:28), and is oriented, shall we say, to a horizontal movement of spreading outward, the goal of procreation in the second chapter is expressed in what we might call a vertical orientation, implying descent through successive generations. The end envisioned is defeat and destruction of the instigator of human disobedience—not, mind you, the serpent,[9] a form of merely creaturely symbolism, but Satan himself—accomplished by an unnamed but particular descendant of the woman.

Here we discover the true significance of the fact that the woman's punishment was imposed before that of the man. It is not because she was being singled out as the sole cause of all the misery that followed in the wake of the Fall (as has often been alleged), for the man was equally implicated along with her. The real reason is that her punishment had to do directly with the fulfillment of the destiny just decreed for the serpent.

---

9. Nor, we should emphasize, does it portend the destruction of his offspring—that is, those who submit to his lies and therefore show that he is their father (John 8:39–47)—for they are human beings who are objects of God's mercy to the very end.

It is none other than her offspring who will accomplish the divinely-declared purpose of bruising his head, that is, dealing him the final and fatal blow. For her to have offspring, however, she must give birth, and now that it has been decreed that that birth will necessarily entail suffering, suffering becomes the divinely-appointed means by which the victory must and will be won.

Surely, we might say, the woman's anatomy could have been designed in such a way that the act of giving birth would not have had the capacity of causing her pain in the first place. Now we can see why this is not the case. It appears that she was not so designed in view of the divinely-foreseen need for redemption, which would come only through an arduous process extending over multiple generations. The Fall, therefore, did not introduce suffering into the world, because suffering was part of mortal existence for humankind in its natural state. We note that God does not say to the woman, "I will give you pain," but "I will multiply your pain in childbearing" (Gen 3:16). Instead, the Fall caused her pain to be intensified, and more importantly, to be embodied in a salutary way—that is, as the means of her salvation.[10]

Here we can see how merciful and providential God was in his response to the original sin. He addressed first of all its instigator, the serpent, with his decree that, while it would inflict a grievous wound on the woman's presumably-remote offspring (thereby signaling a generational struggle), that offspring would, in the end, mortally wound the serpent (foreshadowing ultimate victory). Only then did God turn to the woman whose role it would be to provide the offspring by which, through the course of generations, that victory would finally be won. It would come only, he implies, through suffering—suffering borne on her part by the very act of producing those generations required for the achieving of that victory. Thus not only was suffering re-introduced into the world in the form of pain that had the highest possible purpose—the triumph of humankind over its primordial adversary—but it was forever associated with the hope of the renewal of the whole cosmos.[11]

---

10. It seems likely that this is the background for St. Paul's assertion that "the woman" (referring, in the context, to Eve) "will be saved through childbearing" (1 Tim 2:14–15).

11. In coming to this conclusion, it may seem that we are suggesting that suffering is, in itself, a good. This is true only inasmuch as it is a necessary means to a good end, in which case the evil of suffering is co-opted, as it were, and appropriated in the divine purpose to serve the good: deliverance (or delivery, in the language of childbirth) from sin and death.

In the previous state of innocence and probation, as a result of the divine amelioration of the natural pains involved in childbirth, the woman did not have to suffer inordinately in pregnancy and delivery. But now, in consequence of her disobedience, God tells her, "in pain you shall bring forth children" (Gen 3:16). While the reference here may be primarily to the act of giving birth, all the discomforts and hardships of the entire term of pregnancy itself for the woman are doubtless included in the pronouncement. For our purposes, therefore, birth pangs are generally to be understood in the broad sense of pain associated with the childbearing process.

The sentence was indeed grievous, but it was given in light—and in fulfillment—of God's promise to deliver the man and the woman, and all their descendants, however many they might prove to be, from the power of their common enemy. The suffering entailed had its very origin in God's love for the humanity made in his image, as well as in the love of man and woman for each other. Above all, it was pain with a purpose—and this, we submit, makes all the difference.

Birth Pangs in All Suffering

It is news to no one—especially mothers—that birth pangs are a form of suffering, but what is not sufficiently well understood is that, *mutis mutandis*, suffering itself is a form of birth pangs.

Surely it is no coincidence that, in the biblical telling of the aftermath of the Fall, the initial imposition of suffering on human beings should be in the form of pain the unique quality of which is intrinsically regenerative—its sole cause and purpose being the bringing of new life into the world. We have seen that its ultimate end appears to be beyond (we now know, far beyond) the birth of a child to Eve. In fact, that end turns out to be the bringing into the world of a man (*anthropos*, John 16:21). Penultimately, this is "the man Christ Jesus," the "one mediator between God and men" (1 Tim 2:5), and ultimately, it is what St. Augustine called the "one man" or the "whole Christ,"[12] consisting of Jesus as the head and the Church—or the company of all the redeemed—as his body. Henceforth, therefore, all suffering of whatever kind will, in God's plan, partake of the nature of birth pangs.

The truth of this is borne out by what God goes on to say and do after decreeing punishment for the serpent and the woman. He proceeds

---

12. Kenneth, *From the Fathers*, 1159.

to assign punishment to the man as well. "Because you have listened to the voice of your wife," he says to Adam, "and have eaten of the tree of which I commanded you, 'You shall not eat of it,' cursed is the ground because of you; in pain you shall eat of it all the days of your life; thorns and thistles it shall bring forth for you . . . By the sweat of your face you shall eat bread, till you return to the ground'" (Gen 3:17–19).

The suffering of the woman was assigned to her as a particular kind of labor, and now, so too is the man's. His suffering, however, is linked to the kind of physical labor entailed in an effort to procure food.

The man's suffering thus partakes of the nature of birth pangs in its own peculiar way and within its own distinctive sphere. He is to contribute to the bringing forth of children by sustaining the woman in her pregnancy and providing the food necessary for her vitality, nourishment, and strength, as well as for the child's essential developmental growth. While the woman supplies the nurturing womb within which new life can grow and develop, the man provides the protective environment wherein mother and child are kept safe and well. The hardship involved in actually giving birth is indeed experienced by the woman alone, but because she and the man are "one flesh" (Gen 2:24)—he shares not only in that hardship, but also in its result.[13] His suffering for her sake and for the child therefore becomes his participation in her birth pangs, and as a consequence, birth pangs for him as well.

In speaking of pain, we should be clear that we have in mind not just its physical manifestation, but its mental, psychological, and spiritual forms, as well. If pain can be generalized as whatever hurts, then suffering is the enduring of that hurt. Another way of putting this is that suffering is whatever pain in our lives we must be patient with—patience (Latin *patientia*, from *patior*, to suffer, endure) being, after all, another way of saying suffering. Certainly, we do not have in mind merely trivial instances such as being forced to wait in line at the grocery store or at a stop light, or figuratively having to bite our tongue when someone else is speaking. We mean the enduring—either voluntarily or by necessity—of discomfort and hardship.

The sheer magnitude of such suffering in the world is, of course, staggering. Just on a physical level, probably at least twenty percent of the earth's population at any given time is experiencing some level of hunger

---

13. In the same way, while the hardship involved in obtaining food may historically have been borne primarily by men, women too have shared in it.

or thirst, and equal numbers are undergoing discomfort associated with extreme heat or cold. Bodily aches and pains afflict virtually everyone in some degree, with a significant portion of the world's population experiencing chronic maladies, diseases, and conditions that subject them to constant and often excruciating hurt. Wounds and injuries of every sort and seriousness, whether occasioned by carelessness or malice, human warfare or natural catastrophe, are an ongoing source of profound dysplasia for untold multitudes of people.

Add to all of this the mental and psychological afflictions that beset many in pathological ways, and most—if not all—of us incidentally but with regularity. And then there are, necessarily, the griefs and sorrows that attend our disappointments, rejections, and failures: broken relationships, addictions of various kinds, and mistreatment at the hands of others, not to mention all the anxieties and worries for ourselves and others that continuously plague our minds and disturb our consciences. All this pain occasions our sufferings and constitutes that which—while we rightly seek to alleviate it—we find ourselves, nevertheless, for the most part, forced to endure and be patient with.

In the secular worldview, the pain and suffering that we have described are simply the natural and inevitable concomitant of sentient existence in a world of inherent conflict. Nature is, as Alfred, Lord Tennyson, put it, "red in tooth and claw"[14]; humanity is engaged, according to Thomas Hobbes, in a "war of all against all"[15]; and Charles Darwin's "survival of the fittest"[16] entails a perpetual battle with its inexorable logic of winners and losers. It is, in short, the way things always have been and always will be.

The Judeo-Christian worldview, on the other hand, posits both a beginning and an end to pain and suffering. There was a time when it was not, and there will come a time when it will be no more. This is possible only because pain and suffering bear within themselves the seeds of their own dissolution. "Unless a grain of wheat falls into the earth and dies," Jesus tells his disciples, "it remains alone; but if it dies, it bears much fruit" (John 12:24).

Such falling into the ground and dying is, we submit, in the divine intention, birth pangs. That is, it is oriented by God ultimately to the

---

14. Tennyson, *In Memoriam* (1850), Canto 56.

15. *Bellum omnium contra omnes* (Hobbes, Preface to *De Cive*, 1642).

16. An expression coined by Herbert Spencer (*Principles of Biology*, 1864, 1:444) to describe Darwin's concept of "natural selection" (*On the Origin of Species*, 1859).

INTRODUCTION: SUFFERING AS BIRTH PANGS

redemption of the old creation and the bringing forth of the new. But—and this is an extremely important caveat—whether these birth pangs have their intended result depends on the alignment with God's purposes of those who suffer. To that point, we note that St. Paul's promise that "all things work together for good" is qualified in two significant ways: firstly, for "those who love God," and secondly, for "those who are called according to his purpose" (Rom 8:28).

In other words, not all suffering leads ultimately to the desired outcome. In the natural order, after all, it is well-known that not all birth pangs lead successfully to live birth. Just as a pregnant woman can miscarry—through no fault whatsoever of her own—or her children be still-born as the outcome of her labor, so can human sufferings in general be frustrated in the attainment of their divinely-intended goal.

Here we must make a critical distinction between those who suffer in and for Jesus and those who suffer apart from or in opposition to him. To speak in general terms, the suffering of the former, which is "for doing good" (1 Pet 3:17) "according to God's will" (1 Pet 3:19), is fruitful, not only in the end but also along the way, while the suffering of the latter, "for doing evil," if maintained to the end, is finally fruitless—without, however, we must hasten to add, ever losing its character as birth pangs.

Jesus himself described these two categories of people in terms of what he called healthy and diseased trees (Matt 7:17–20). Healthy trees are people who are fruitful, he says, because of their acceptance of him: they "enter by the narrow gate" (Matt 7:13), are "known" by him (Matt 7:23), and "hear his words and do them" (Matt 7:24). Diseased trees, by the same token, are those who are ultimately barren because—and so long as—they reject him. Their sufferings are birth pangs for them potentially, but become such actually only if and when they align themselves with God's purposes. Failure to do this results in their suffering being finally understood ruefully by them as birth pangs that lead not to live- but to still-birth.

Moreover, if, in the case of healthy trees, fruit can be understood in terms of the manifestation of Jesus—that is, his being brought into the world through birth pangs—then there are obviously gradations of fruitfulness depending on the nature of the sufferings that are experienced. The most fruitful sufferings in this regard are those that are the direct result of living for and testifying to Jesus. These are the sufferings, for instance, of Christian martyrs throughout history, who have, by their willingness to give their lives for love of God, revealed the character of

Christ to the world. Christ himself is seen and known in those who suffer unto death for his sake, for they conform their testimony to his. The first martyr, St. Stephen, is exemplary in this regard. As he is being set upon by his persecutors, he says, "Behold, I see the heavens opened, and the Son of man [that is, Jesus] standing at the right hand of God" (Acts 7:56). Before he dies, he evokes Jesus's final request of the Father on the cross—"Father, forgive them, for they know not what they do" (Luke 23:34)—when he falls to his knees and cries out with a loud voice, "Lord, do not hold their sin against them" (Acts 7:60).

Those who suffer in lesser ways for the sake of Jesus, the gospel, or the Church are also especially fruitful. St. Paul (who would himself, of course, eventually be martyred) is the best example of this kind of fruitfulness. "Remember Jesus Christ, risen from the dead, the offspring of David, as preached in my gospel, for which I am suffering," he writes to Timothy. "I endure everything for the sake of the elect [the baptized], that they also may obtain the salvation that is in Christ Jesus with eternal glory" (2 Tim 2:8–10). For the sake of "Christ Jesus my Lord," he solemnly affirms elsewhere, "I have suffered the loss of all things" (Phil 3:8).

It is notable that Paul himself sees these sufferings as a form of birth pangs that he must undergo. "My little children," he addresses the Galatians, "for whom I am in the anguish of childbirth until Christ is formed in you!" (Gal 4:19). Clearly, according to him, it is the lot of others as well to suffer in this way. "It has been granted to you," he writes to the Philippians, "that for the sake of Christ you should not only believe in him but also suffer for his sake" (Phil 1:29).

Indeed, the sufferings of the martyrs and all those who endure hardship on Jesus's behalf are, according to the Scriptures, a participation in the sufferings of Christ himself. We must, however, be careful about how we understand this. It cannot mean that we somehow share vicariously in the pains that Jesus endured in his earthly life—and particularly on the cross—for those have long since ceased. Nor can it mean that the risen and glorified Lord, who is forever beyond the personal experience of pain, is currently suffering in heaven what we are undergoing as his people on earth. This is a misunderstanding of Jesus's self-identification to St. Paul on the road to Damascus ("I am Jesus whom you are persecuting," Acts 9:5), which would make Jesus himself currently subject to the slings and arrows of his enemies.

INTRODUCTION: SUFFERING AS BIRTH PANGS

To share in the sufferings of Jesus is, in actuality, to share his attitude to his sufferings. In other words, it is to think about our sufferings as he did of his—in short, to "have this mind among yourselves, which is yours in Christ Jesus" (Phil 2:5). That mind in regard to suffering is best shown in words Jesus speaks to his disciples in the upper room before his Passion. "When a woman is giving birth," he says to them, "she has sorrow because her hour has come, but when she has delivered the baby, she no longer remembers the anguish, for joy that a human being has been born into the world" (John 16:21). Any doubt regarding to whom he is referring is removed when he goes on to say in his prayer to the Father that "the hour has come" (John 17:1), that is, the time of his Passion, his giving birth.[17]

Jesus's sufferings are thus, to him, birth pangs, and so ought ours to be for us. St. Paul "has Christ's mind" in him (1 Cor 2:16), and so he can, like Jesus, "rejoice in my suffering," and not only that, but also "in my flesh fill up what is lacking in Christ's afflictions for the sake of his body, that is, the Church" (Col 1:24). The implication is that the sufferings of Jesus do not, by themselves, bring to fruition the new creation that is being birthed. The birth pangs of the old creation are encapsulated in his, but ours must, in the outworking of the divine plan, be added to them before they issue in the promised new heavens and new earth.

What, though, can we say of those pains "healthy trees" experience that are not traceable, at least directly, to their witness to Jesus? What, in other words, of all the sufferings that Christians share as the common lot of humanity? In what sense can they too be birth pangs? The answer is, quite simply, according to H. Wheeler Robinson, that they are what they are believed to be. "Suffering in itself," he writes,

> has no moral value. It is, so to speak, so much raw material of life. We cannot say what suffering means to a spiritual being till we know what will be his attitude towards it. It may make a man better or worse, as we say; but that will depend entirely on what he himself does with it. It may sweeten his nature or embitter it, according to his own reaction to it. Similarly, though *mutatis mutandis*, the suffering of God will derive its significance from his attitude to it. That attitude might have been one simply of holy retribution to the cause of the suffering, but if it had been that, and nothing more, we should never have had the Christian conception of God. The characteristic feature of that conception is grace, and

---

17. See chapter 2.

grace here means the voluntary acceptance of the suffering in the working out of the divine purpose to save.[18]

It is, in other words, our accepting attitude toward suffering in general that determines, not only its bear-ability, but also its fruitfulness. The reality is that we have to live with it, for better or for worse. For worse is to fight it, to rail against it, to "kick against the goads" (Acts 26:14). For better is to embrace it, to internalize our pain as pangs, our sufferings as birth pains. When we do this, we become more patient, more joyful, more positive, more hopeful, more expectant, not unlike a laboring mother anticipating the approaching birth of her child. In that case, what is said of a pregnant woman—"she is expecting"—becomes true of us, as well.

In short, while suffering for the sake of Jesus is, we might say, birth pangs by definition, our ordinary hurts and pains are birth pangs by transmutation. This happens solely as a consequence of our attitude toward them. Just as we ourselves must be "transformed by the renewal of [our] mind[s]" (Rom 12:2), so must our pain be transformed. "When we become aware that we do not have to escape our pains," writes Henri Nouwen, "but that we can mobilize them in a common search for life, those very pains are transformed from expressions of despair into signs of hope."[19]

If we come to see all our pain as birth pangs, its tolerance and endurance becomes the occasion—and even the source—of hope and joy. St. Paul's view of suffering as birth pangs, noted above, surely lies behind these words of his to the Romans: "We rejoice in our sufferings, knowing that suffering produces endurance, and endurance produces character, and character produces hope" (Rom 5:3-4). Examples of this way of thinking on the part of New Testament writers may be multiplied (Heb 11:11; Jas 1:2-3; 1 Pet 1:6-7; 4:13).

We have said that Jesus identifies himself in his Passion with a woman giving birth. But he surely intends the disciples to whom he speaks, and by extension, the Church of which they are the nucleus, to see themselves—by virtue of the fact that they are "in me" (John 14:20)—in her, as well. All those who are members of that Church, therefore, are that woman, called to see themselves in travail, and to regard their sufferings in this world as the pangs of childbirth, a gift given to them that they might be God's surrogates to bring forth that human being—"the man Christ Jesus" (1 Tim 2:5)—into the world.

18. Robinson, *Suffering Human and Divine*, 182.
19. Nouwen, *Wounded Healer*, 95.

INTRODUCTION: SUFFERING AS BIRTH PANGS

One Generation to Another

It is no coincidence that suffering is first presented in the Scriptures in connection with labor: the woman laboring in giving birth, the man laboring in providing food. Both are curses that will be providentially turned into blessings, as redeemed humanity must "work out [its] own salvation with fear and trembling" (Phil 2:11–12). Because birth pangs are an inalienable part of the human condition after the Fall, we may say that they are, in a sense, co-extensive with human history. Indeed, we can go so far as to say that they are the very stuff of that history inasmuch as history itself depends on the continuation of the race through successive generations.

In the biblical account, as we have said, the suffering of the man is attached to the sustenance of the human race. In contrast, it is to the propagation of the race that the woman's suffering is tied. Had humanity remained in its pristine, unfallen state, that propagation would presumably have had, as we have suggested, a fundamentally horizontal dimension or orientation. That is to say, its end would have been a spreading out and peopling of the earth, in keeping with God's original command to fill it (Gen 1:28). However, while propagation continues to fulfill that function after the Fall, at that point its primary, eschatological[20] orientation shifts to the vertical, that is, more particularly, to a single line of descent through generations.

In contrast to Adam's suffering, Eve's—and that of her female descendants—will be for the sake of ensuring the propagation of the race through time. If each successive generation is to be sustained by the man's labor,[21] the very succession of the generations will depend on the labor of the woman. All this is to serve the primary end that, through those generations, the offspring of the woman might at last be enabled, in "the fullness of time" (Gal 4:4), to overcome its adversary and redeem humankind from sin and death.

The genealogies painstakingly recorded throughout the Scriptures—summed up, in their significance, in the opening chapters of St. Matthew's and St. Luke's Gospels—bear repeated witness to this downward and directed movement. In keeping with the traditional patriarchal concept of ancestry, they are invariably couched in terms of fatherhood rather than motherhood. "Abraham was the father of Isaac," Matthew begins

---

20. Having to do with the End, or *Eschaton*.

21. This is in no way to denigrate women's historical contribution to labor's sustaining of life, but only to draw out the contrast implicit in the assignment of punishments following the Fall.

(Matt 1:1), and Luke starts his genealogy, "Jesus . . . being the son (as was supposed) of Joseph" (Luke 3:23). This highlights the man's role in the begetting of offspring—admittedly indispensable, but also momentary and pleasurable. At the same time, however, it regrettably obscures the woman's part, which is, in contrast, both prolonged and painful. In this hidden way, birth pangs are the unspoken presupposition of the multigenerational engine, if you will, that drives not only history itself but the salvation that is divinely embedded in it. In our very existence, we and all our forebears are each and every one the product of pain.

It is precisely in and through this succession that we should expect to find the end, or purpose, for the original imposition of birth pangs. Only in that context, in fact, can we clearly see that the punishment imposed on the woman for her role in the original act of disobedience in the Garden of Eden actually bears within itself the germ or seed of blessing of which we have spoken. In its initial form of birth pangs, therefore, suffering itself is in a very real sense given the end to which, in the providence of God, it will be adapted to serve. It just so happens that this end is providentially foreshadowed in the birth and subsequent histories of Eve's first two children, related in the fourth chapter of Genesis.

On the one hand, the story of Cain's murder of Abel can be seen as simply a reiteration of the Fall[22]—the transgression of Adam and Eve being repeated in their offspring. This interpretation is lent credence by the pronouncement on Cain for the killing of his brother of a punishment identical to that given to his father. "Now you are cursed from the ground" (Gen 4:11; 3:17–19), God tells him, after Cain has spilled Abel's blood into it. While this inference may be true, it does not by any means exhaust the significance of the brothers' roles. In fact, they play a far more significant part as confirming the fulfillment of God's promise in the fate decreed for the serpent.

In God's original declaration of the promise inherent in the curse pronounced on Eve, we note that the proximity to her of her offspring (the individual descendant of whom we have spoken) is not specified. For all she knows, Cain—her first-conceived child whom she subsequently must labor to bring into the world—could himself be the offspring referred to. This, of course, turns out emphatically not to be the case. By murdering his younger brother, Cain not only disqualifies himself as the offspring of the woman but in effect declares himself to be the offspring of the serpent.

---

22. And therefore also as evidence of the doctrine of original sin.

INTRODUCTION: SUFFERING AS BIRTH PANGS

Nonetheless, despite—or rather on account of—this, Abel, his younger brother—later to be characterized as righteous (Heb 11:4a)—becomes a type or figure of the woman's awaited offspring. By virtue of the fact that his death is at the hands of his older brother, that death foreshadows Jesus's execution by the Romans at the instigation and on the insistence of his fellow Jews. Abel's death, we might say, constitutes the bruising merely of his own heel, especially in view of the fact that, as the writer to the Hebrews says, "he still speaks" (Heb 11:4b).[23] For his part, Cain, standing in for the serpent, is, in a sense, bruised at God's hand by the imposition of a mark, presumably placed on his (fore)head (Gen 4:15). Thus, the fulfillment of both the promise to the woman and the curse on the serpent are, in an anticipatory way, carried out in the very first generation after Adam and Eve, summing up, as it were, the whole sweep of salvation history in advance.[24] As we now know, of course, that history will turn out to be both long and painful.

---

23. The reference being, of course, to the "voice of [his] blood . . . crying to [God] from the ground" (Gen 4:10).

24. We note that, as a sign of God's patience with the offspring of the serpent, while the curse pronounced on the ground for Adam's transgression is reiterated in Cain's case, Cain himself is mercifully protected from the vengeance due him for his brother's murder (Gen 4:15–16).

Chapter 1

The Birth Pangs of Israel

> A great sign appeared in heaven: a woman clothed with the sun, with the moon under her feet, and on her head a crown of twelve stars. She was pregnant and was crying out in birth pains and the agony of giving birth . . . [and] she gave birth to a male child.
> *Revelation 12:1–2, 5*

As Jesus sits on the Mount of Olives, after his triumphal entry into Jerusalem, his disciples ask him, "What will be the sign of your coming and of the close of the age?" (Matt 24:3). He cautions them against expecting either in the near term. "You will hear of wars and rumors of wars," he says, which "must take place, for nation will rise against nation, and kingdom against kingdom, and there will be famines and earthquakes in various places" (Matt 24:6–7). Then he adds something that must have truly startled them: "All these are but the beginning of the birth pains" (Matt 24:8).

To understand their undoubted surprise, we need to bear in mind, first of all, what we have already seen. According to the interpretation given to Genesis 3:15 in biblical tradition, the woman's offspring, who must be birthed through a painful process, is none other than Messiah (*meshiach*), the anointed king who is to be the deliverer of his people, Israel.

The birth pains of which Jesus speaks, then, are a reference to something that would have been familiar to his disciples, as indeed to every Jew of their day. This was the expectation, based on the combination of God's curses pronounced on the serpent and on the woman, that a period of intense suffering—the so-called messianic woes[1]—would precede Messiah's coming. Given, however, that through their spokesman Peter the disciples had acknowledged Jesus himself to be that *Christos*[2] (Matt 16:16), they were surely taken aback to hear that the birth pangs that were to lead up to Christ's coming—which from their perspective had already taken place—were in fact only just about to begin.[3]

As has been shown, the onerous version of birth pangs themselves had its beginning in the Garden of Eden when they were imposed on Eve for her transgression of God's command. It is their progress from that point that now engages our attention, and in that progress we can discern four distinct stages: the travail of Israel, leading up to the angelic annunciation to Mary; the travail of Jesus, terminating in his death on the cross; the travail of the Church corporately and of Christians individually, transpiring in anticipation of Jesus's return in glory; and, prior to the final Judgment, the travail of the cosmos, issuing in the inauguration of the new heavens and new earth.

Our focus in this chapter is on the first of these stages: the messianic woes proper—that is, those birth pangs experienced by God's people, Israel, which serve to bring forth from them, as from a womb, the woman's promised offspring, who is Jesus.

The Pangs of Being Born

It was the firm conviction of all the Jewish rabbis and commentators that, since the bearing of the messianic offspring would necessarily be the occasion of great pain, tribulation would surely precede and attend Messiah's coming. Accordingly, by extension from Eve, the whole people must inevitably suffer in order that Messiah, whom Israel carried, as it were, in her womb, might be brought forth at last to triumph over her enemies.

Seen from this primary perspective, the messianic woes are pre-eminently those suffered by Israel as a mother. To these we will return momentarily. But as we will see, it appears that, as a rule, the one who suffers birth pangs in bearing a child must first be shown to have endured them as

---

1. The *heblo sel masiha* of the rabbis, typically represented in the New Testament by *thlipsis* (tribulation).

2. The Greek equivalent of *meshiach*.

3. We defer until chapter 3 an explanation of what Jesus means by implying that they are yet to come.

LIKE A WOMAN IN TRAVAIL

a child being born. This proves to be the case not only with Israel, but also with Jesus himself (as we will show in chapter 2) and the Church (chapter 3), as well as with individual Christians (chapter 4), and it appears to hold even with the cosmos itself (chapter 5).

As if to foreshadow the woes that her offspring Messiah will have to undergo in his turn—according to the Christian understanding of him as the "suffering servant" set forth in chapters 42 through 53 of the book of Isaiah—Israel the mother, then, must first suffer as a child being birthed.[4] She is depicted elsewhere in the Old Testament, after all, not only as having her Maker as her husband (Isa 54:5), but also—in the context of deliverance from Pharaoh's yoke—as being God's "first-born son" (Exod 4:22). In Egypt this son is, we might say, being gestated in the womb of God, who, like an expectant mother (Deut 32:18) shares his people's sufferings (Exod 2:23–25; 3:7–9). As if to confirm that this is the case, on the very verge of bringing the people forth from Egypt, God commands that henceforth the first-born of every womb should be redeemed and delivered, in commemoration of the impending redemption and delivery of his own first-born (Exod 13:2, 11–16).

We obviously have no way of knowing directly how a child experiences the birth process. However, we can speculate about it, as has one writer: "To the baby being born it must feel like some terrible kind of death as it is wrested from the only sort of life it has known, wrenched from the safety of that enclosed space into the open air, from the security of darkness into blinding light and noise. It cannot possibly know that life in the womb is being exchanged for a life that will be infinitely more rich and free. What feels like the pain of dying may also be the pain of being re-born."[5] It is certainly easy to see that the violent contractions of the womb experienced as birth pangs by the mother may also very well be experienced by the child as pains of being born. These contractions produce wave-like undulations in its fetal sac, causing the child—after the woman's waters break—to be expelled from the womb and carried down, by means of struggle, through the constricting birth canal.

Such pains are analogous to what we witness the Israelites undergoing in the course of their deliverance from Egypt, which ultimately led to their

---

4. An allusion to such suffering may possibly be found in Hos 13:13, where it is said that the pangs of childbirth come for Ephraim (Israel), who is pictured as waiting in the womb.

5. De Waal, *Living with Contradiction*, 123.

emergence as a nation in the Sinai desert (Exod 19:4–6). In addition to the plagues that preceded and accompanied their departure (Exod 7:14—12:32) they had to endure what must have been a terrifying ordeal in crossing the Red Sea to emerge on the far side (Exod 14:21–29). In the first place, the wind that drove back the sea all through that night was howling above and around them. And then, as they passed over on dry land, the walls of water to right and left of them could not have been but be a menacing sight, and must have seemed at any moment ready to come crashing down. Their passage through the sea was fraught with peril and danger, and was no doubt accomplished in something like panic, especially in view of the fact that the chariots of the pursuing Egyptians were not far behind.

It would appear that there is evidence in the national consciousness of Israel as it has been imprinted on the Old Testament literature to suggest that the experience itself of crossing the Red Sea became a powerful metaphor for birth, or re-birth.[6] It is striking, for instance, how often watery imagery is used to convey feelings of distress, especially in the Psalms. This leads us to suspect that its origin is traceable to some water-related experience embedded in the collective memory of the people, of which the most obvious candidate is the crossing of the Red Sea.

The experience described by the writer of Psalm 88 may serve as an example of the way in which this imagery is applied. The soul of the psalmist is "full of troubles," and his life "draws near to Sheol" (Ps 88:3). He is "counted among those who go down to the pit" (Ps 88:4), "like one set loose among the dead" (Ps 88:5). Furthermore, he complains to God that "you have put me in the depths of the pit, in the regions dark and deep. Your wrath lies heavy upon me, and you overwhelm me with all your waves" (Ps 88:6–7). The choice of words appears calculated to conjure up the image of a drowning person. We feel the darkness, the struggle, the suffocation and choking—even the lungs beginning to fill with water. He concludes: "Afflicted and close to death from my youth up, I suffer your terrors; I am helpless. Your wrath has swept over me; your dreadful assaults destroy me. They surround me like a flood all day long; they close in on me together" (Ps 88:15–17).

The motif of waves rolling and breaking overhead is widespread in the so-called psalms of lamentation (Pss 18, 32, 42, 69), where drowning is

---

6. In this tradition St. Paul speaks of the passage "through the sea" as a form of baptism (1 Cor 10: 1–2).

"merely figurative for death."⁷ These psalms abound in references to being saved from many (Ps 18:16), great (Ps 32:6), or deep (Ps 69:1–2) waters, or from the flood (Ps 69:14–15). "All your breakers and your waves have gone over me," complains the psalmist (Ps 42:7). Jonah's cry of distress "from the belly of the fish" (Jonah 2:1) captures the feeling of desperation and abandonment well:

> I called to the LORD, out of my distress, and he answered me; out of the belly of Sheol I cried, and you heard my voice. For you cast me into the deep, into the heart of the seas, and the flood surrounded me; all your waves and your billows passed over me... The waters closed in over me to take my life; the deep surrounded me; weeds were wrapped about my head at the roots of the mountains. I went down to the land whose bars closed upon me forever; yet you brought up my life from the pit, O LORD my God. (Jonah 2:3, 5–6)

All this, and especially Jonah's subsequent expulsion from the belly of the fish onto the shore (Jonah 2:10)—surely far from a pleasant experience—can be read as a kind of birthing process.⁸ Paul Tillich argues that depth psychology offers a partial explanation for the strong power that the elements (in particular, water, for instance, in baptism) exercise over us. He points out that "water, on the one hand, is a symbol of the origin of life in the womb of the mother, which is a symbol for the creative source of all things, and... on the other hand, it is a symbol of death—the return to the origin of things."⁹

The womb itself is a watery environment, and the child within it might be characterized as a sort of submerged swimmer. "The beginning of every life," one observer writes, "is a lonely fight with death."¹⁰ "Our very birth and entrance into this life," says seventeenth-century Anglican priest and poet John Donne, "is an issue from death, for in our mother's womb we are dead, so as that we do not know we live, not so much as we do in our sleep."¹¹

---

7. Sasson, *Jonah*, 202.

8. According to Jonah's own description, the fish's actual belly (Hebrew *meʿ eh*, inward parts) represents the figurative belly (*beten*, womb) of Sheol (Jonah 2:2)—that is, the grave, or death—and therefore his emergence from it is a form of resurrection: "the sign of the prophet Jonah" (Matt 12:40).

9. Tillich, *Protestant Era*, 104.

10. Houselander, *Passion of the Infant Christ*, 52.

11. Donne, "Death's Duel," 212.

The Pangs of Pregnancy

We turn now to Israel's experience of birth pangs as a mother, which is the proper reference of the messianic woes.

Why, we may begin by asking, should human procreation entail a period of gestation in a womb in the first place? The obvious answer, from a physical point of view, is that the fetus needs time to grow and develop in order to reach viability in the outside world. In divine revelation, however, it is evident that spiritual realities are often embodied in physical arrangements, a prime example of which is the mystery of the relationship between Christ and his Church which St. Paul discovers between husband and wife in the sacrament of Holy Matrimony (Eph 5:25–32). We might venture the assertion, then, that physical gestation during pregnancy speaks in an analogous way of a period of preparation prior to the manifestation of Messiah to the world in the person of Jesus, born in the "fullness of time" (Gal 4:4) to the Virgin Mary. We can actually discern three such periods in the bringing forth of Messiah.

The beginning of the first, unlike the other two, is not temporal—that is, it does not take place in time. As the Nicene Creed affirms on the basis of St. John's use of the term *monogenes* (only-begotten) to describe Jesus in his pre-incarnate state (John 1:14, 18; 3:16, 18; 1 John 4:9), the Son of God is "begotten of the Father before all ages." He dwells, as it were, in the womb of eternity, the place of hiddenness between begetting and birth, where his temporal bringing forth can be prepared.

The Father speaks of his corresponding birth as a kind of second begetting, this time temporal in nature. "You are my Son," he says in the second psalm; "today I have begotten you" (Ps 2:7). The historical reference here is apparently to David's anointing as king (1 Sam 16:13; 2 Sam 2:4; 5:3; Ps 89:26–28). This must be interpreted, however, in light of what another messianic psalm says about the king's Lord. "From the womb of the morning," the psalmist claims, "the dew of youth will be yours" (Ps 110:3). We surmise that the beginning of this new day is none other than the first day of creation, when God said, "Let there be light" (Gen 1:3). Indeed, this is precisely what we may suppose Jesus is ultimately referring to when he says, "I have come into the world as light, so that whoever believes in me may not remain in darkness" (John 12:46). The birth here, then, is none other than what St. Paul alludes to when he calls Christ "the firstborn of all creation" (Col 1:15). Thus the first period of so-called gestation—that of the Father's eternal Son—is book-ended, so to speak, by eternal begottenness, on the one hand, and the beginning of time in creation, on the other.

The begetting that initiates the second gestational period we have in mind is the begetting of Israel herself by Abraham, her father. If Levi, one of Jacob's twelve sons, can be said figuratively to have been originally "in the loins of Abraham" (Heb 7:11), then surely the same is also potentially true of all eleven of his brothers, and therefore of Israel herself, because together they—the original "children of Israel" (that is, of Jacob)—were the nucleus of the nation. Accordingly, Israel took its beginning in and with Abraham, the first of its patriarchal fathers, who—to adopt the language of the genealogies—begot the nation through Isaac and Jacob.

The miraculous manner of the conception of Isaac, when Abraham was in his old age (Gen 21:2) and Sarah was past the age of childbearing (Gen 17:17; 18:12), is foreshadowed by the equally miraculous conception of faith in the patriarch's heart. God frequently appeared to Abraham and spoke to him (Gen 12:1; 13:14; 17:1; 18:1; 22:1), but on one occasion alone is this self-revelation described as a coming to him of a "word of the Lord": "'Fear not, Abram, I am your shield; your reward shall be very great.' But Abram said, 'O Lord God, what will you give me, for I continue childless . . . ? Behold, you have given me no offspring, and a member of my household will be my heir.' And behold, the word of the Lord came to him: . . . '[Y]our very own son shall be your heir'" (Gen 15:1–4). It is no coincidence at all that the begetting of a multitude of descendants as many as the stars of heaven (Gen 15:5) was made dependent on Abraham's ability to father but one child by his wife. Nor is it a coincidence that, at precisely this point, Abraham was said to believe the Lord (Gen 15: 6). That is, he believed that God would fulfill his promise—his word—to him.

For his part, the Lord's subsequent act of counting this act of believing to Abraham as righteousness (Gen 15:6) is, among other things, a way of saying that the Lord's word—a divine seed (1 Pet 1:23)—had been mystically planted within him. This seed would, in turn, bear fruit through Sarah in the form of Isaac, whose birth foreshadowed the birth of Jesus, both of them being "children of the promise" (Rom 9:8). Thus does the second period of Messiah's gestation extend from the time of Abraham to Jesus himself,[12] the period *par excellence* of the messianic woes, our primary interest in this chapter.

---

12. Coinciding with the range of the genealogy in St. Matthew's Gospel (Matt 1:1–17).

This brings us, finally, to a third period, the gestation of Messiah in the womb of the blessed Virgin, a gestation which also serves as the culmination of the pregnancy of Israel. Once more there is a divine begetting, this time of the Son of God in human form. At the Annunciation, Gabriel says to Mary, "The Holy Spirit will come upon you, and the power of the Most High will overshadow you" (Luke 1:35), and "you will conceive in your womb and bear a son, and you will call his name Jesus" (Luke 1:31). The moment of this begetting—this immaculate conception on the part of the Virgin—is the moment of the Incarnation, when the Word who is God (John 1:1) becomes flesh—a human being—and dwells among his people (John 1:14). He has to grow and develop within his mother like any other child, and after nine months descend through the birth canal and be brought forth into the world.

Of these three gestations, it should be noted, only the second involves birth pangs. For obvious reasons, the first—the gestation of the eternally-begotten Son "in the bosom of the Father" (John 1:18) prior to his coming forth as light at the inception of creation—does not entail pain on the Father's part. The painlessness of the third gestation, however—of Jesus in and from the womb of the blessed Virgin—is not self-explanatory.

On this matter, the Scriptures are silent, but as the fruit of her reflection on the mystery of the Incarnation, the Church teaches that, in a miraculous way, Mary did not experience the pangs of childbirth when Jesus was born. In order to understand this, we must remember that, in the state of innocence, Eve was—by divine dispensation of a supernatural gift—to be spared the natural pain that accompanied the birth of children. The Virgin received a like dispensation through the bestowal upon her of the extraordinary grace of divine favor, announced by the angel: "Greetings, O favored one,[13] the Lord is with you!" (Luke 1:28). Moreover, just as Eve saw the pain of giving birth not only reinstated but also intensified as pangs due to her disobedience, so through Mary's obedience in saying, "Behold, I am the servant of the Lord; let it be to me according to your word" (Luke 1:38), was she formally exempted from the throes involved in giving birth under the reign of sin and death.

---

13. Greek *kecharitomene*, traditionally translated "full of grace."

The Gestation of Messiah in Israel's Womb

One way of stating Israel's vocation is to say that she was charged with the bringing forth of Messiah. When God is finally ready to make this calling explicit, he does so by choosing the insignificant village of Bethlehem Ephrathah as her surrogate. "From you," he goes on to say, "shall come forth for me one who is to be ruler in Israel, whose coming forth is from of old, from ancient days" (Mic 5:2). The culmination of this coming forth is said to be "when she who is in labor has given birth" (Mic 5:3), thereby connecting the prophecy to the promise of an offspring to Eve. As it turns out, the birth-mother here proves to be none other than Mary, in her role as the representative of God's people.

It would appear that St. John the Divine has precisely this prophecy in mind when he describes what he calls "a great sign" that appeared in heaven: "a woman clothed with the sun, with the moon under her feet, and on her head a crown of twelve stars," who "was pregnant and was crying out in birth pains and the agony of giving birth, [and] . . . gave birth to a male child" (Rev 12:1–2, 5). But we have just said that Mary did not suffer in giving birth to Jesus. If this is true, how can this woman, depicted as enduring such travail, be identified with her? The answer lies in seeing Mary's person as conflated with her people, the people of Israel, whose vocation she epitomizes as the mother of Israel's Messiah.[14]

While, as we have seen, Mary personally did not have the normal maternal experience in giving birth to Jesus, the reality is that Israel had already endured birth pangs for her. All of the sufferings of the people, from the days of Abraham right up to the massacre of all the male children by King Herod at the time of Jesus's birth (Matt 2:16), were, in fact, the birth pangs of Messiah, the fabled messianic woes.[15] Actually, these pangs are, we might say, recapitulated, or brought to a head, in the suffering of those innocent children and their families at Herod's hands. When St. Matthew relates the massacre, he ascribes it to the fulfillment of a prophecy of Jeremiah regarding Jacob's wife Rachel, who died in giving birth to her son Benjamin "when her labor was at its hardest" (Gen 35:16–19). "A voice was heard in Ramah, weeping and loud lamentation," Matthew quotes the

---

14. LeFrois, *Woman Clothed with the Sun*, 259.

15. We make a distinction between these and the human sufferings of Jesus himself, including all those that he endured during his ministry, which were not part of the messianic woes proper. As we will see in chapter 2, his personal sufferings—and particularly those of his Passion—represent the travail involved in birthing the Church.

prophet: "Rachel weeping for her children; she refused to be comforted, because they are no more" (Matt 2:18; Jer 31:15).

Mary's suffering is a part of this—indeed, as we have said, it is the culmination of it—but her suffering is not to be traced, as we might expect, to the cave in Bethlehem. Rather, it comes at the cross on Golgotha,[16] where her son is decisively declared, by the placing of an inscription—"Jesus of Nazareth, the King of the Jews" (John 19:19)—over his head, to be the ruler promised by Micah for Israel. Here, indeed, as Simeon had prophesied, does a sword "pierce through [her] own soul also" (Luke 2:35).

In his vision, after all, St. John tells us that, immediately after the woman brings him forth, "her child was caught up to God and to his throne" (Rev 12:5). This confirms that the birth in question is not the nativity of Jesus but rather his Passion–resurrection, immediately following which he ascends to the Father.[17] In this case, the birth pangs and agony experienced by the woman John sees are, on the one hand, to be associated with the sufferings of Jesus on the cross,[18] and on the other, to be identified with the recapitulation, or summing up, as it were, of Israel's sufferings in Mary's vigil at the foot of that cross as she watches her beloved son die an excruciating death (John 19:25).

Prophetic Pangs

The most striking testimony to the equation of Israel's suffering with birth pangs comes from the books of the Prophets. The simile "like a woman in labor" occurs once in the Psalms (Ps 48:6) but no fewer than thirteen times in various forms throughout the prophetic writings (Isa 13:8; 21:3; 26:17; 42:14; Jer 4:31; 6:24; 13:21; 22:23; 30:6; 49:24; 50:43; Hos 13:13; Mic 5:2). The repeated invocation of the pains associated with pregnancy and childbirth to express the sufferings of the nation as a whole gives these pains an exemplary status. "Even in the male-dominated society of the Old Testament," says one commentator, "the suffering of childbirth

---

16. Feuillet, *Johannine Studies*, 263.

17. The final ascension of Jesus to heaven does not take place until forty days after his resurrection (Acts 1:3), but he expressly alludes to an imminent departure during his appearance to the first witnesses (John 20:17). At any rate, we have here, in the chronology of St. John the Divine's vision, an example of the prophetic foreshortening of time.

18. See chapter 2.

was proverbial to evoke the idea of supreme anguish."[19] At the same time, the comparison provided the primary impetus for the imagery of the messianic woes that would be taken up in earnest by the apocalyptic writers of the intertestamental period.

To begin with, there is evidence in the oldest strata of the tradition underlying the Old Testament literature that birth pangs became shorthand for great anguish at a very early period. In the undoubtedly archaic "song of Moses" (Exod 15:1–18), celebrating the Israelites' victory at the Red Sea after the exodus from Egypt, we read this paean to the Lord: "You have led in your steadfast love the people whom you redeemed; you have guided them by your strength to your holy abode. The peoples have heard; they tremble; pangs[20] have seized the inhabitants of Philistia. Now are the chiefs of Edom dismayed; trembling seizes the leaders of Moab; all the inhabitants of Canaan have melted away. Terror and dread fall upon them; because of the greatness of your arm" (Exod 15:13–16; Deut 2:25). Such metaphorical pangs were clearly the worst of inward pains, suffered by those who anticipated what this mighty God might do to them through the people whom he was now bringing in their direction.

It is in the Psalms that we first find the explicit comparison of human suffering to the pangs that accompany childbirth. This too occurs in the context of the dread that is brought upon God's enemies who contemplate his greatness and power: "Behold, the kings assembled; they came on together. As soon as they saw it, they were astounded; they were in panic; they took to flight. Trembling took hold of them there, anguish as of a woman in labor" (Ps 48:4–6).

When we turn to the Prophets, we meet the same comparison with regularity. To give just one example, speaking of the Babylonians at the approach of the "day of the Lord," Isaiah says, "They will be dismayed: pangs and agony will seize them; they will be in anguish like a woman in labor. They will look aghast at one another; their faces will be aflame" (Isa 13:8). The prophet himself is subject to their onset, presumably on behalf of doomed Babylon:

> As whirlwinds in the Negeb sweep on, it comes from the wilderness, from a terrible land. A stern vision is told to me; the traitor betrays, and the destroyer destroys. "Go up, O Elam; lay siege, O

---

19. Vawter, *On Genesis*, 84.

20. "Pangs" here represents, as elsewhere, the Hebrew consonant cluster *h-b-l*, which is in turn rendered in the Septuagint as *odinas*.

Media; all the sighing she has caused I bring to an end." Therefore my loins are filled with anguish; pangs have seized me, like the pangs of a woman in labor; I am bowed down so that I cannot hear; I am dismayed so that I cannot see. My heart staggers; horror has appalled me; the twilight I longed for has been turned for me into trembling. (Isa 21:1–4)

Jeremiah, the so-called "weeping prophet," also experiences pangs, but in solidarity with Israel herself rather than in relation to her adversaries: "For the wound of the daughter [Jerusalem] of my people is my heart wounded; I mourn, and in my perplexity *birth pangs as of a woman in childbirth overwhelm me*" (Jer 8:21[21]). Thus does the metaphor begin to express the depths of the corporate experience that will come to be characterized as the messianic woes. "I heard a cry as of a woman in labor," Jeremiah says, "anguish as of one giving birth to her first child, the cry of the daughter of Zion gasping for breath, stretching out her hands, 'Woe is me! I am fainting before murderers'" (Jer 4:31). And again, at the approach of the Babylonians, we read: "Thus says the LORD: 'Behold, a people is coming from the north country, a great nation is stirring from the farthest parts of the earth. They lay hold on bow and javelin; they are cruel and have no mercy; the sound of them is like the roaring sea; they ride on horses, set in array as a man for battle, against you, O daughter of Zion!' We have heard the report of it; our hands fall helpless; anguish has taken hold of us, pain as of a woman in labor" (Jer 6:22–24).

The prophet Micah also takes up the lament: "And you, O tower of the flock, hill of the daughter of Zion, to you it shall come, the former dominion shall come, kingship for the daughter of Jerusalem. Now why do you cry aloud? Is there no king in you? Has your counselor perished, that pain seized you like a woman in labor? Writhe and groan, O daughter of Zion, like a woman in labor, for now you shall go out from the city and dwell in the open country; you shall go to Babylon" (Mic 4:8–10).

It falls to the prophet Isaiah to struggle with the complications of his people's pregnancy. Speaking on behalf of the Lord, he rebukes those who question what God is doing in the life of the nation: "Woe to him who strives with him who formed him, a pot among earthen pots! Does the clay say to him who forms it, 'What are you making?' or 'Your work has no handles'? Woe to him who says to a father, 'What are you begetting?' or to a woman,

---

21. The italicized words are our own translation from the Septuagint. In the English Standard Version, the second half of the verse is rendered "dismay has taken hold on me."

'With what are you in labor?'" (Isa 45:9–10). The Lord himself, it would seem, is this father who has begotten Messiah, whom Israel, as this woman, labors to bring forth. But—according to Hosea—like his mother, this child (the people as God's son) is stubborn, and refuses to be born. "The iniquity of Ephraim[22] is bound up; his sin is kept in store. The pangs of childbirth come for him, but he is an unwise son, for at the right time he does not present himself at the opening of the womb" (Hos 13:13).[23]

Isaiah betrays his frustration: "O LORD, in distress they sought you; they poured out a whispered prayer when your discipline was upon them. Like a pregnant woman who writhes and cries out in her pangs when she is near to giving birth, so were we because of you, O LORD; we were pregnant, we writhed, but we have given birth to wind. We have accomplished no deliverance in the earth" (Isa 26:16–18). Israel must suffer, the prophet concludes, but God will finally deliver her of her child, and it is he who will have the last word: "'Before she was in labor she gave birth; before her pain came upon her she delivered a son.' Who has heard such a thing? Who has seen such things? Shall a land be born in one day? Shall a nation be brought forth in one moment? For as soon as Zion was in labor she brought forth her children. 'Shall I bring to the point of birth and not cause to bring forth?' says the LORD; 'shall I, who cause to bring forth, shut the womb?' says your God" (Isa 66:7–9).

A remarkable passage from the Dead Sea scrolls sheds light on the way Messiah's birth was conceptualized in this tradition. "I was in distress as a woman in travail bringing forth her first child," personified-Israel recounts in this literal translation from a Qumran document.

> for [her] birth pangs came suddenly and an agonizing pain with her birth-throes to cause writhing in the womb of the pregnant woman, for children are come to the waves of death and she who conceived a male child was distressed by her pains, for with the waves of death she shall be delivered of a man-child and with infernal pains there shall break forth from the womb of the pregnant woman a wondrous counselor,[24] in his might and there shall come

---

22. An alternative designation for Israel.

23. This passage from Hosea has been cited in the introduction as a possible allusion to the pains experienced by a child in the process of being brought to birth.

24. Dupont-Sommer (*Essene Writings from Qumran*, 207–8) points out that this is the same designation of Messiah as is found in Isa 9:6.

forth safely a male child from the throes of birth by the woman who was pregnant with him. (QH3 37:7–10).[25]

The Messianic Woes in Apocalyptic Writings

A brief interlude of several hundred years intervened between the eclipse of the prophets (approximately 200 BCE) and the fulfillment of God's promise to bring forth Messiah, the offspring of the woman, from Israel at "the time of the end" (Dan 12:4). If the whole history of the nation to that point, in terms of her sufferings, may be likened to her pregnancy, this latter period proves to be the time of the onset of her labor pains in earnest.

Certainly, the people as a whole, already reduced to client status under the oppressive rule of the Greek Seleucids and Ptolomies, experienced a crisis during the mid-second century BCE that threatened to extinguish its very existence. Antiochus Epiphanes IV, execrated by the Jews for his antipathy to their law and customs, over-ran Jerusalem and placed a pagan altar—"the abomination of desolation" (Matt 24:15) "spoken of by the prophet Daniel" (Dan 9:27)—in the temple, provoking the Maccabean wars. This conflict between the besieged nation and its Gentile adversaries occasioned a vivid description of the messianic woes in the form of so-called apocalyptic[26] writings, beginning with the canonical book of Daniel and drawing on the imagery of birth pangs that we have found to be pervasive in the Prophets.

If, as one commentator has written, "the whole messianic idea was the inevitable outcome of the history of afflictions which beset Israel from the beginning of its national existence,"[27] now the nation and the rest of mankind appeared to be heading into a final conflagration, and the apocalyptic authors, according to another writer, "looked for the end of the world to be preceded by a time of unprecedented suffering."[28] "Many of the Jewish texts that foretell the end of the present world order," therefore, says Dale C. Allison Jr., "also announce the coming of a great tribulation,

---

25. Baumgarten and Mansoor, "Studies in the New *Hodayot*," 189–90.
26. "Unveiling."
27. Klausner, *Messianic Idea in Israel*, 441.
28. Rowley, *Relevance of Apocalyptic*, 171.

a final time of trouble that is to mark the transition between this age and the age to come."[29]

The stereotyped descriptions of this catastrophic period—characterized by earthquakes, famines, wars, droughts, persecutions, and signs and portents in the heavens—were to culminate in the revealing of Messiah and the final judgment. They are best known to Christians through the so-called eschatological discourses delivered by Jesus and recorded in all three synoptic Gospels (Matt 24:3–51; Mark 3:3–37; Luke 21:10–36). Interestingly, according to Allison, their occurrence is not always depicted in the apocalyptic literature as a present reality. In other words, the significance that they have is by no means exhausted in the circumstances of Israel in the second and first centuries BCE.[30] Sometimes, he says, they are pending, in which case, as we will suggest in chapter 2, they are fulfilled in the lifetime of Jesus, and particularly in the events surrounding his Passion. Sometimes they are manifested at an unspecified time, easily equated with two millennia (and counting) of Church history (chapters 3 and 4), especially as characterized in the book of Revelation. And sometimes they are reserved until a possibly distant time, coinciding with the eschatological travail of the cosmos itself (chapter 5), as described by St. Paul in chapter 8 of his letter to the Romans.

---

29. Allison, *End of the Ages*, 5.

30. Allison, *End of the Ages*, 19. In fact, as we have already intimated and will see in chapter 3, Jesus himself in effect takes and transfers them to the future, making them woes to be experienced by the Church in the world between his departure and his second coming.

Chapter 2

The Birth Pangs of Jesus

> This Jesus, delivered up according to the definite plan and foreknowledge of God, you crucified and killed by the hands of lawless men. God raised him up, loosing the pangs of death, because it was not possible for him to be held by it. *Acts 2:23–24*

WE HAVE SEEN THAT the messianic woes, experienced as birth pangs by Israel through her long history, fulfill their purpose and reach their formal conclusion with the birth of Messiah and the associated slaughter of male children in Bethlehem. Messiah's nativity—as Jesus (Luke 1:31)—is, we might say, his first birth, which, in this instance, is literally a "birth from above" (John 3:5). As such, it is of course the pre-condition necessary if he is to give birth in his turn, in keeping with the pattern we have observed in the case of Israel. But we will see that, in his unique case, Jesus himself must, in a manner of speaking, be born again—that is, re-born—as the Christ (Acts 2:36) if he is truly to be the mother that we will postulate him to be.

We may legitimately wonder if Jesus suffers in being birthed by Mary. On the one hand, we have observed[1] that a child leaving the protective environment of the womb and undertaking the short journey through the birth canal likely experiences considerable stress and discomfort. If, on the other hand, by being "blessed among women" (Luke 1:42), Mary is spared her share of pangs in giving birth to Jesus, we might safely assume that Jesus—himself the beloved Son with whom the Father declared himself to

---

1. See chapter 1.

be well pleased (Luke 3:22)—is also exempted from whatever pains may be involved in being brought into the world.

If this is true, then in much the same way that Mary's birth pangs are both vicariously experienced by Israel on her behalf and reserved for her as a sword-thrust through her soul at the foot of the cross, so the pains of being born are for Jesus deferred to the course of his earthly life *post-partum* and, in their excruciating culmination, as he hangs from that same cross. From this perspective, therefore, his earthly life becomes his gestation, and his Passion, his delivery. In this way, and not solely by his brief sojourn in Egypt as a child (Matt 2:13–15), does Jesus's entire life re-enact and recapitulate the four-hundred-year bondage of Israel, God's firstborn son (Exod 4:22), in Egypt leading up to the dramatic deliverance at the Red Sea. As God says, "When Israel was a child"—here we take the liberty of picturing him yet in the womb—"I loved him, and out of Egypt I called my son" (Hos 11:1).

Thus, from the point of view which (as we will see) was taken by St. Peter after the Resurrection, Jesus himself is brought to a second birth through the pangs of death (Acts 2:24). Subsequently, too, he is, on the one hand, "declared to be the Son of God in power according to the Spirit of holiness by his resurrection from the dead," according to St. Paul (Rom 1:4), and on the other, thereby designated by the apostles as God's *pais* (child), according to St. Luke (Acts 3:13, 26; 4:27, 30). Simultaneously, however, a second and complementary perspective to this emerges, that of Jesus as a mother who labors on the cross to bring forth her own children, the Church. We will attempt to explicate these two ways of understanding Jesus's sufferings one at a time, beginning with the former.

Jesus Being Birthed

In his earthly existence, our Lord may be characterized as a man of sorrows (Isa 53:3), and with good reason. "It is well known," says Church of England bishop Launcelot Andrewes, in a sermon preached on Good Friday in 1605,

> that Christ and his cross were never parted, but that all his life long was a continuous cross. At the very [manger], his cross first began. There Herod sought to do that which Pilate did, even to end his life before it began. All his life after, saith the apostle, was nothing but a perpetual "gainsaying of sinners" [Heb 12:3], which we call "crossing" . . . In the psalm of the Passion, the

twenty-second, in the very front or inscription of it, he is set forth unto us under the term of a [deer], "a morning hart," a hart roused early in the morning; as from his birth he was by Herod, and hunted and chased all his life long.[2]

"The whole life of Christ was a continual Passion," John Donne asserts in one of his sermons on the feast of the Nativity. "Others die martyrs, but Christ was born a martyr. He found a Golgotha (where he was crucified) even in Bethlehem, where he was born . . . His birth and his death were but one continual act, and his Christmas Day and his Good Friday are but the evening and morning of one and the same day."[3] "The swaddling bands were the first burial bands," says one contemporary writer; with his birth, "the Passion had begun."[4] Another has put it this way: "If the Passion, in its historical reality, took place in less than twenty-four hours, in its spiritual reality it spanned [Jesus's] entire life."[5]

In one of his sermons, nineteenth-century Anglican priest John Keble thus summarizes Jesus's life of woe:

> Our Lord's first humiliation of himself was in a manner repeated in all his doings upon earth: in his lowly birth; in his persecuted childhood; in the poverty and obscurity of his youth; in the wanderings, labors, cares, sorrows, fears, the blasphemy and reproach and all the contradiction of sinners, which he willingly endured all the time of his ministry. Every instance of that kind was a sort of shadow and figure of the first great humiliation: God made man; and the whole was completed on the awe-ful and saving cross. His whole life in every part of it, every one of his mysterious mercies and sufferings, looks backward to his incarnation, and forward to his cross.[6]

It is on the cross, indeed, that Jesus's earthly sufferings were finally revealed as what they truly represented: birth pangs. What St. Peter says in his first post-Pentecostal sermon is key to understanding this: "Men of Israel, hear these words: Jesus of Nazareth, a man attested to you by God with

---

2. Kenneth, *From the Fathers*, 499.
3. Donne, "Showing Forth of Christ," 76.
4. Houselander, *Reed of God*, 59.
5. Gabriel, *Divine Intimacy*, 398. Indeed, as early as the third century, St. Cyprian, in his *Treatise on the Lord's Prayer*, goes even so far as to say that it was "in the glory of [the] blood" of Abel, who "was the first to bear the witness of martyrdom," that the Lord's Passion had its true beginning (Kenneth, *From the Fathers*, 415).
6. Kenneth, *From the Fathers*, 666–67.

mighty works and wonders and signs that God did through him in your midst, as you yourselves know—this Jesus, delivered up according to the definite plan and foreknowledge of God, you crucified and killed by the hands of lawless men. God raised him up, loosing the pangs of death, because it was not possible for him to be held by it" (Acts 2:22–24).

In the first place, St. Peter's reference to the "mighty works and wonders and signs" performed by Jesus evokes the miraculous deliverance of the Israelites at the time of the exodus—a deliverance which constituted, as we have seen,[7] the pangs of being birthed for Israel, God's first-born son. What is most significant for our purposes, however, about these words of Peter (the first preserved for us of those uttered publicly about the death and resurrection of Jesus) is the fact that to the statement of the most stupendous sign of all, his resurrection, Peter appends a kind of gloss that gives a glimpse of what we might call, for lack of a better term, the mechanism of this miracle. In raising Jesus to life, he says, God is also at the same time loosing what he calls "the pangs of death." We must take time to unpack the significance of this expression.

The phrase "pangs of death" (*odinas tou thanatou*) is a quotation from the Greek translation of the Psalms, where it appears in the Septuagint as *odinas thanatou* (Pss 17:5; 114:3).[8] The word *odinas* is the plural form of the feminine noun *odin*, which stands—as previously pointed out—for not just any pangs or pains but for a very particular kind: those felt by a woman while giving birth to a child. The fact that few translations bring this out obscures the real significance and meaning of the expression. The term itself is a remarkable one, opening up the possibility that the Passion and death of Jesus can themselves be characterized as birth pangs.

But what is perhaps even more remarkable is the textual emendation that has brought about that characterization in the first place. In the original Hebrew of both psalms that we have cited, the word that is translated by the Greek *odinas* is *heble*, which means "bonds" or "cords," connoting the restrictive or confining nature of death. How, then, has this notion of death ensnaring and holding captive its victim become transmuted into the imagery of birth pangs? The answer to this question must be found on two levels.

---

7. In chapter 1.

8. In the English Standard Version, Pss 18:5a and 116:3, respectively. Compare the parallel phrase *odinas hadou*, "pangs of hades [death]" (Ps 17:6, ESV 18:5b).

On the level of language, the shift appears to be quite simply the result of a misreading by the Septuagint translator. The Hebrew consonants *h-b-l* that form the basis of *heble* can actually represent two different words, depending on the vowels with which they are read. At the time the Septuagint translation was made, between 250 and 200 BCE, words—which in Hebrew are comprised solely of consonants—were not vocalized or "pointed" in the written text of the Hebrew Bible, and so vowels had to be supplied, as it were, by the reader, either from memory or from hints in the context as to the implied use and meaning of any given word.[9]

It seems that the translator of Pss 18:5-6 and 116:3 from Hebrew into Greek construed the consonants *h-b-l* with vowels that required the word to be understood, not as bonds (*heble*) but as birth pangs (*hebel*). Thus enshrined in the Septuagint, it was this reading that provided St. Peter with the language that he used to characterize the death and resurrection of Jesus.[10]

However, the deeper, existential cause of the transformation from bonds to birth pangs is found in the conversion—we might even call it a "providential reversal"[11]—of death itself that has been effected by the sacrificial dying and rising again of Jesus, with the consequence that death-as-bonds has been changed into death-as-birth pangs. The subsequent resurrection of Jesus is evidence of and testimony to this overcoming—even reversal—of death's power. Having entered the tomb, Jesus straightway converts it into a womb from which he can then emerge, "the firstborn from the dead" (Col 1:18).

Looking back on Israel's history, we find numerous illustrations of these so-called providential reversals. One of the most outstanding is certainly the story of Joseph, told in the concluding chapters of the book of Genesis. First thrown into a waterless pit by his brothers and then sold into slavery in Egypt, where he is cast into prison due to the false accusation of his master's wife, Joseph rises to become Pharaoh's chancellor and Egypt's governor. In that capacity he becomes the savior of his family from the famine that grips his homeland in his absence. As he explains to his brothers, "you meant evil

---

9. It was not until approximately the ninth century CE that vowel pointings were added to the text by rabbinical scholars.

10. Peter almost certainly spoke to his fellow Jews in Aramaic, so the rendering of his words in Greek is most likely to be attributed to St. Luke, the narrator. Nonetheless, we are justified in assuming that Luke has faithfully represented their original sense.

11. For this expression I am indebted to A. R. Knapp, who coined it for a teaching given in November, 1983.

against me, but God meant it for good, to bring it about that many people should be kept alive, as they are today" (Gen 50:20).

A different sort of reversal is found in the account of Balak, a Moabite king, and Balaam, a diviner or prophet. Fearing the approach of the Israelites to his desert kingdom, Balak hires Balaam to pronounce a curse on them, but God forbids it because, he says, "they are blessed" (Num 22:12). When Balaam persists, the curses he intends to utter come out of his mouth as blessings instead. Later writers of Scripture interpret this as an instance of the Lord's "turn[ing] the curse . . . into a blessing" (Deut 23:5; Neh 13:2). By redeeming his people, God is even said to change them from a curse into a blessing: "As you have been a byword of cursing among the nations, O house of Judah and house of Israel, so will I save you, and you shall be a blessing" (Zech 8:13).

The idea that God not only can do such a thing as this but actually operates this way throws new light on the first curse imposed by the Lord—on the serpent and, through the serpent, on humanity itself. Those who argue that there is no room in the pronouncement of punishment on the serpent for a promise of blessing to man[12] simply overlook this aspect of the Hebrew's conception of his God. The seed, so to speak, of blessing is latent within the curse itself. The serpent will strike the heel of the man's offspring, and that offspring will die as a result, but his death will crush the serpent's head, destroying its power and thereby delivering "all those who through fear of death were subject to lifelong slavery" (Heb 2:15). All that remains is for death itself, imposed on the man and woman for their transgression of the command not to eat of the tree of the knowledge of good and evil, to be abolished (2 Tim 1:10) by its conversion into a kind of birth.

Resurrection to incorruptible life is both the ultimate reversal of the prototypical curse—death—and its final transformation into blessing. The "death of [the Lord's] saints" goes from being "costly" (*yaqor*) in the Hebrew of Psalm 116:15—reflecting the prevailing view of that time that death severed all ties between God and man—to "precious" (*timios*) in the Septuagint under the intervening influence of the emerging belief in the doctrine of resurrection. It is true that "the LORD sustains [the one who considers the poor] on his sickbed" (Ps 41:1), but he also does more: "in his illness [God turns] all his bed" (Ps 41:3, ESV margin). This transformation of the sick man's bed—to which we might relate the command of Jesus to the paralytic to "pick up your bed, and go home" (Mark 2:11)—is

---

12. Westermann, *Genesis 1–11*, 260.

analogous to the conversion of tomb into womb. All other such reversals—for example, weeping into joy (Ps 30:5), ashes into "a beautiful headdress," mourning into "the oil of gladness," a faint spirit into "a garment of praise" (Isa 61:3), sorrow into joy (John 16:20)—are not only responses to, but consequences of, this fundamental conversion.

It is on this basis that the believer, whatever his or her circumstances, can take heart and have hope. St. Paul exemplifies this attitude when he writes to the church at Philippi from a Roman jail: "I want you to know, brothers, that what has happened to me has really served to advance the gospel, so that it has become known throughout the whole imperial guard and to all the rest that my imprisonment is for Christ. And most of the brothers, having become confident in the Lord by my imprisonment, are much more bold to speak the word without fear" (Phil 1:12–14). The original Greek is even more to the point. Paul's "imprisonment" is literally a "bond" (*desma*), or fetter, that shackles him, much the same way that we have seen death's bonds encompass the psalmist. When it becomes known that they are "for Christ," they too are transformed into birth pangs, which by being loosed are productive of new life.[13]

St. Paul not only finds that his imprisonment is no longer the impediment, or curse, that his readers naturally expect, but discovers that it has been transformed into precisely the opposite: an actual impetus—or blessing—to his work. "A strange chemistry of providence this," comments Matthew Henry, "to extract so great a good as the enlargement of the gospel out of so great an evil as the confinement of the apostle."[14]

When Jesus rises from the dead, the Gospel accounts make clear that it is the women most closely and most immediately associated with the vigil at the cross (Matt 27:55–56; Mark 15:40–41; Luke 23:49; John 19:25) and the burial (Matt 27:61; Mark 15:47; Luke 23:55–56) who are also the ones to take to others the word about the empty tomb (Matt 28:1–10; Mark 16:1–9; Luke 24:1–8; John 20:1–2, 11–18). This has a special poignancy and appropriateness if it is true that Jesus has, by rising, turned that tomb into a womb. As putative child-bearers themselves, these women are eminently and uniquely qualified to testify to a resurrection conceived as the emergence of offspring from this womb.

---

13. We note, moreover, that an earthquake unlooses the bond (*desma*, Acts 16:26) holding Paul and Silas in their Philippian jail, just as an earthquake marks the resurrection of Jesus (Matt 27:51).

14. Henry, *Bethany Parallel Commentary*, 1164.

Of some interest in this connection is a curious expression used in the description of the high priest's garment in the Pentateuch (Exod 28:32). What is spoken of there as the "woven binding around the opening [for the head]" is literally, in Hebrew, "like the opening of a womb." The head of the high priest passing through it in the act of putting it on, therefore, may be seen as analogous to that of a child emerging headfirst from the womb, and perhaps points us to the emergence of "the man Christ Jesus" (1 Tim 2:5), who is our "great high priest" (Heb 4:14), from the womb of the grave in his resurrection.

It is this conversion—death into birth pangs, the tomb into a womb—that testifies to the immense power which is exerted in the resurrection of Jesus, a power figuratively expressed in the words of St. Peter when he says that, in raising Jesus to life, God loosed him from the pangs of death. Having converted death into birth pangs, God demonstrates his power and control over them precisely by causing them to cease in the act of bringing forth Jesus to a new level of life. One writer has put it this way: "In Acts 2:24, the reference is to the birth of the Messiah, or rather to new birth through the resurrection . . . God himself has relieved the pangs of birth out of death. The abyss can no more hold the redeemer than a pregnant woman can hold the child in her body. Under severe labor pains the womb of the underworld must release the redeemer. God himself helps it to end the pains."[15] As in the case of a woman in labor, the contractions of this womb expel the child, and then, having served their painful purpose, come to a provisional end.

We are reminded once more of the death of Jacob's wife Rachel in childbirth, as it is recorded in the book of Genesis. She "went into labor," the narrator says, and "when her labor was at its hardest, the midwife said to her, 'Do not fear, for you have another son.' And as her soul was departing (for she was dying), she called his name Ben-Oni, but his father called him Benjamin" (Gen 35:16–18). "Ben-Oni" means "son of my sorrow," an apt description of Jesus dying on the cross from Mary's point of view as his mother. "Benjamin," the new name given to him by Jacob, signifies "son of the right hand," pointing forward to the "name that is above every name" bestowed on Jesus by his Father when he raised him from the dead and "highly exalted" him to his right hand in heaven, "so that at the name of Jesus every knee should bow, in heaven and on earth and under the

---

15. Bertram, "*Odin/odino*," 673.

earth, and every tongue confess that Jesus Christ is Lord, to the glory of God the Father" (Phil 2:9–11).

Jesus Giving Birth

We have maintained that, depending on the perspective that we adopt, Jesus's birth pangs can be seen as either the pains that he undergoes in being brought through death to birth, or alternatively, the pangs that he endures in bringing a child to birth. It is to the second of these perspectives that we now turn our attention.

Here we are invited to contemplate Jesus as a mother—a task which, on its face, may strain both our credulity and our imagination. After all, he is a male human being who lacks precisely the reproductive organs necessary for conceiving and bearing children, as well as for experiencing the pangs involved in giving birth. God himself, however, is often spoken of by the biblical writers in mothering terms. Under the old covenant, he is likened to "an eagle that stirs up its nest, that flutters over its young, spreading out its wings" (Deut 32:11; Ps 91:4). He is said to be "the God who gave you birth" (Deut 32:18), one who "cries out like a woman in labor" (Isa 42:14), and like a woman who can't forget her nursing child (Isa 49:15).

By the same token, Jesus likens himself to "a hen [that] gathers her brood under her wings" (Luke 13:34). His compassion is invariably expressed in the Gospels by the word *splagchnizesthai*, applied only to him (Matt 9:36; 14:14; 15:32; 20:34; Mark 1:41; 6:34; 8:2; 9:22; Luke 7:13) or to those clearly intended to represent him (Matt 18:27; Luke 10:33; 15:20). This verb (from *splagchna*, inward parts, entrails) is best rendered literally as "to be wrenched in the gut," a plausible way of characterizing the abdominal pain of a woman in labor.

This visceral feeling is brought out most vividly in St. John's account of the visit of Jesus to the grave of his friend Lazarus. "When Jesus saw [Mary, the sister of Lazarus] weeping," St. John tells us, "he was deeply moved in his spirit and greatly troubled" (John 11:33) and openly wept (John 11:35). It does not require much imagination to read what follows as a kind of childbirth. "Then Jesus, deeply moved again, came to the tomb. It was a cave, and a stone lay against it. Jesus said, 'Take away the stone'" (John 11:38–39). After offering a prayer to his Father, "he cried out with a loud voice, 'Lazarus, come out,'" and "the man who had died came out" (John 11:43-44). In more ways than one, this was a rehearsal for what Jesus would experience on the cross.

It is, after all, on that cross that Jesus suffered most profoundly, and it is there that we should expect to find him experiencing the climax of his own birth pangs. He himself signaled this, appropriately enough, to those women who mourned and lamented for him as he was being led out to be crucified. "Turning to them," St. Luke tells us, "Jesus said, 'Daughters of Jerusalem, do not weep for me, but weep for yourselves and for your children. For behold, the days are coming when they will say, "Blessed are the barren and the wombs that never bore and the breasts that never nursed!"'" (Luke 23:27-29). While, on the one hand, he foresaw times of great suffering ahead for God's people, on the other, he counted himself as under a kind of curse because of what he had to undergo in order to be fruitful.

It should not surprise us that Jesus's maleness proved to be no hindrance at all to prevent medieval commentators—especially those who happened to be women—from openly contemplating his maternity. While the image of feeding on the Eucharist from Jesus's breast is found in the Church fathers as early as the end of the second century,[16] St. Anselm of Canterbury (1033-1109) appears to have been the first to speak of what we might call the reproductive aspect of Jesus's Passion. "It is by your death that [we] have been born," he writes in the form of a prayer, "for if you had not been in labor, you could not have borne death; and if you had not died, you would not have been brought forth. For, longing to bear sons into life, you tasted of death, and by dying you begat them."[17]

It is, however, a woman, Marguerite of Oingt, a French Carthusian nun and mystic (1240-1310), who took up this theme and made the comparison of Jesus on the cross to a woman in labor more explicit:

> O sweet and lovely Lord, how bitterly were you in labor for me all through your life! But when the time approached where you had to give birth, the labor was such that your holy sweat was like drops of blood which poured out of your body onto the ground . . . O sweet Lord Jesus, who ever saw any mother suffer such a birth! But when the hour of birth came you were placed on the hard bed of the cross where you could not move or turn around or stretch your limbs as someone who suffers such great pain should be able

---

16. Clement of Alexandria, *The Instructor*, 6.
17. Anselm, *Prayers and Meditations*, 153.

to do ... and surely it was no wonder that your veins were broken when you gave birth to the world all in one day.[18]

It was left to the English anchoress Julian of Norwich (1343-1416) to speak overtly of Jesus as a mother in his Passion and death. "We know," she says, "that all our mothers bear us for pain and death," and goes on: "But our true Mother Jesus, he alone bears us for joy and for endless life, blessed may he be. So he carries us within him in love and travail, until the full time when he wanted to suffer the sharpest thorns and cruel pains that ever were or will be, and at last he died. And when he had finished, and had borne us so for bliss, still all this could not satisfy his wonderful love."[19] His hands and feet affixed to the wood before it is raised up to be thrust into the ground, the cross becomes the bed alluded to by Marguerite of Oingt upon which Jesus goes into labor. Like a woman in travail, he cries out with a loud voice, "My God, my God, why have you forsaken me?" (Matt 27:46; Mark 15:34) and "I thirst" (John 19:28), at which point the soldiers "put a sponge full of sour wine on a hyssop branch and held it to his mouth" (John19:29) to deaden the pain. "When Jesus had received the sour wine," St. John writes, "he said, 'It is finished,' and he bowed his head and gave up his spirit" (John 19:30). In St. John's Gospel, as Thomas Andrew Bennett has notably said, "Jesus's response to crucifixion would be more appropriate to the experience of a woman giving birth than to a man being tortured to death."[20]

Significantly, in his account St. Mark calls attention at this moment once more to the presence of women, both those who followed Jesus and ministered to him when he was in Galilee, and also many other women who came up with him to Jerusalem (Mark 15:40–41). Once more, as presumptive child bearers themselves, these women were empathetic witnesses to the agony through which he had gone and which for them—unlike for Mary, herself spared the pains of parturition in giving birth to Jesus—was reminiscent of the maternal sufferings many of them had no doubt endured.

In Jesus's capacity of being birthed, we have likened him to Rachel's child, Benjamin. But in his labor on the cross, Jesus is like Rachel herself, who dies as a result of giving birth (Gen 35:19). We must turn to St. John in order to understand what it was that he was bringing forth. That is set out for us in the form of two images, one given immediately before Jesus dies

---

18. Blumenfeld-Kosinski, *Writings of Marguerite of Oingt*, 31.
19. Colledge and Walsh, *Julian of Norwich*, 297–98.
20. Bennett, *Labor of God*, 45.

and the other in the moments immediately after, both pointing ahead to, and foreshadowing, the emergence of the Church.

The first image is of Mary and the beloved disciple—certainly to be identified with St. John himself—standing at the foot of the cross. "When Jesus saw his mother and the disciple whom he loved standing nearby," we are told, "he said to his mother, 'Woman, behold, your son!' Then he said to the disciple, 'Behold, your mother!' And from that hour the disciple took her to his own home" (John 19:26–27).

We have said[21] that Mary's birth pangs are deferred to this moment, and that it is here—in the imagery of the vision St. John later describes in the book of Revelation (Rev 12:1–6)—that she brings forth the child whom we have identified with Jesus in his resurrection. But by reporting Jesus's address of her as "woman" and by coupling her with this disciple, the evangelist here rather evokes Mary's association with Eve, the "mother of all living" (Gen 3:20).

We have already commented[22] on the fact that Eve initially bore two sons, Cain and Abel, the first of whom killed the second and then was banished from the family. But we often forget that she had a third child, Seth, whose birth is described by Eve herself as a kind of replacement for the murdered Abel. "God has appointed for me another offspring instead of Abel," she says, "for Cain killed him" (Gen 4:25). As we have seen, Abel is a type of Jesus, that is, he foreshadows him in view of the similarities between them. He is recognized by the writer of the letter to the Hebrews to be righteous (Heb 11:4), as is Jesus by the centurion who, observing the manner of his death, declares, "Certainly this man was innocent[23]" (Luke 23:47). Moreover, as Jesus is put to death by his kinsmen (Acts 2:23, 26), so is Abel by his brother, and the "sprinkled blood" of Jesus "speaks a better word than the blood of Abel" (Heb 12:24), which, God tells Cain, "is crying to me from the ground" (Gen 4:10).

In much the same way, then, that Seth replaces Abel as Eve's son, so now, by Jesus's own bequeathal, does John replace Jesus as Mary's son when Jesus is taken away from her by his death on the cross. Thus do Jesus's pangs, by referral to Mary, result in the figurative birth of an offspring—the beloved disciple (representing, we might say, all other

---

21. In chapter 1.
22. See introduction.
23. *Dikaios*, righteous.

disciples)—who will, in time, crush under his feet the head of Satan (Rom 16:20), whom Jesus by his death has mortally bruised.[24]

The second birthing image, also provided by St. John, is complementary to the first. After Jesus bows his head and gives up his spirit, the evangelist tells us that, in order to confirm his death, "one of the soldiers pierced his side with a spear, and at once came out blood and water" (John 19:34). These substances are universally recognized to be symbolic, respectively, of Eucharist and Baptism, sacraments that are constitutive of the Church.[25]

As Eve is taken from the side of Adam while he is in a deep sleep (Gen 2:21–22), so the Church is brought out of the side of Jesus by a spear-thrust as he sleeps in death. "It was from his side," says St. John Chrysostom, "that Christ formed the Church, as from the side of Adam he formed Eve . . . Just as then he took the rib while Adam was in a deep sleep, so now he gave the blood and water after his death."[26] "God made Eve of the rib of Adam," writes seventeenth-century Anglican theologian Richard Hooker, "and his Church he frameth out of the very flesh, the very wounded and bleeding side of the Son of man."[27]

In her capacity as the new Eve, therefore, Mary both is the mother of the Church—"of all living"—according to the first image, and represents the Church, according to the second. Either way, having given birth to Jesus painlessly in Bethlehem, she vicariously experiences the birth pangs that Jesus endures on Golgotha, the "sword [piercing] through [her] own soul also" (Luke 2:35).

The objection may be raised here that we are asserting that Jesus gives birth before he himself is birthed in resurrection, in contradiction to the pattern that we have observed of the mother being born before she in turn bears her child. As we will see,[28] however, the realities to which the two images associated with Jesus's death point come to fruition only after he rises from the tomb. Jesus's resurrection remains the indispensable pre-condition for the birth of the Church. St. Matthew is, in effect, acknowledging this when, after saying that "tombs . . . were opened" by the earthquake coinciding with Jesus's death on the cross (Matt 27:52), he

---

24. We have suggested in the introduction that this is foreshadowed by the fate of Cain himself (Gen 4:8–16).

25. *Catechism of the Catholic Church*, 201–2

26. Kenneth, *From the Fathers*, 296.

27. Kenneth, *From the Fathers*, 774.

28. In chapter 3.

hastens to add that it is only after his resurrection that "many bodies of the saints who had fallen asleep were raised" (Matt 27:53)

It must be pointed out in conclusion that, apart from the Resurrection (which, as we have contended, represents the emergence of the newborn), the new nature of the tomb as a womb can be neither contemplated nor understood. It is, after all, by passing through the tomb—that is, by dying, being buried, and rising again—that Jesus converts it into a womb. This explains the fact that the book of Job, that great Old Testament meditation on the mystery of suffering, assigned that mystery in the end to the absolute inscrutability of God's purposes (Job 42:1–6). Although Job himself appeared to have had an intimation of it (Job 19:25–27), the doctrine of bodily resurrection from the dead had not yet been clearly revealed.

Chapter 3

The Birth Pangs of the Church

All these are but the beginning of the birth pains. Matthew 24:8

We have maintained that the birth of the Church as the result of Jesus's birth pangs on the cross is foreshadowed under two sets of imagery. One, derived from the creation of Eve from Adam's rib, takes the form of the elements that issue from his pierced side, signifying the sacraments of Holy Baptism and Holy Eucharist, and the other, related to the replacement of Abel by Seth, is represented by his entrusting of the beloved disciple to his own mother.[1] When we consider them separately, we see the birth to which they both refer presented under different but complementary aspects.

On the one hand, the outflow from Jesus's side on the cross, symbolically tied as it is to Eve's formation from Adam, points us toward what we might call the mystical view of the Church's birth, understood in this context to apply to the whole gestational process—taking place in a hidden way—from original conception to final delivery. From this perspective, the Church as the body of Christ is, throughout her history, being formed within him, only to appear finally at the consummation. It remains, as it were, inside his nurturing womb, constantly renewed there by the waters of Baptism and continuously nourished by the blood of the Eucharist.

The mutual committal of Mary and John, on the other hand, in addition to bestowing a new motherhood on the blessed Virgin, forms the nucleus of the new community that Jesus promised to create when

---

1. While she is, at the same time, committed into his care.

he gave his disciples the new commandment that they love one another (John 13:34). This flesh-and-blood community, also the Church, is the earthly anticipation of the emergence of its mystical counterpart. It finds its inception as a body when the risen Christ breathes upon his disciples gathered in the secrecy of the upper room and says to them, "Receive the Holy Spirit" (John 20:22). It is this body that subsequently comes forth into the world (after a foreshortened, fifty-day gestation) on the feast of Pentecost when the Holy Spirit descends publicly upon it (Acts 2:1–4), empowering it to take its first breath, and with that breath, to tell of "the mighty works of God" (Acts 2:11). Henceforth it will grow outwardly even as its counterpart—its *alter ego*, if you will—is growing inwardly.[2]

Both of these developments reach their ultimate goal at the appearance of "the holy city, new Jerusalem, coming down out of heaven from God, prepared as a bride adorned for her husband" (Rev 21:2). This is the Church envisaged in her eschatological glory: in her inward aspect "built as a city" (Ps 122:3), and in her outward aspect clothed with "the fine linen" that is "the righteous deeds of the saints" (Rev 19:8). In the first instance, her descent from heaven—and therefore, out of the womb of the risen and reigning Christ—is like that of a newborn down the birth canal into the light of day, and in the second, that same descent signals her attainment from below to "the measure of the fullness of Christ" (Eph 4:13).

Let us dwell a little longer on each of these simultaneous developments in turn, beginning with the Church seen from the perspective of her growth *in utero Jesu*.

Love's Labor of Building Up

In order to provide the first man with "a helper fit for him" (Gen 2:18), we are told that God took from his side a rib which he "made into a woman" (Gen 2:21–22). In fact, the Hebrew word *banah*, translated "make," has the more nuanced sense of "build," so that, in a literal rendering, "God built the woman" from the man. The act of her being taken from his side represents, therefore, a kind of construction, or building up, that corresponds in the birthing process to the developmental period of gestation

---

2. Although we are describing a Church that is at the same time both visible and invisible, it is not two churches (as in the Calvinist conception) but one. A possible analogy is St. Paul's characterization of the "outer self [*exo anthropos*]" and the "inner [*eso*] self" of a single person (2 Cor 4:16).

in the womb, a time during which outward pangs take rather the corresponding form of inward growing pains.

Under the old covenant, the Lord built up his people—spoken of both as the holy city (Jerusalem) and a daughter (Zion, Isa 52:1–2)—in order that they might be presented to their bridegroom (that is, to himself) and married (Isa 62:4–5). For purposes of the old covenant, this goal was anticipatorily achieved in the immediate presentation of Eve to Adam. Now, however, under the new covenant, the Church as bride finds herself going through the arduous process of being built up in order that she may be brought to her intended bridegroom, Christ.

The key to the Church's growth *in utero* is located in this idea of building up. In the Hebrew, according to one commentator, the root word *banah* "always has to do with 'creating' and 'bringing into existence,'" and "is used to describe the world restored according to the will of God."[3] God's building activity applies, moreover, not only to the natural world but also, in a figurative sense, to families and, understandably, by extension, to houses, or dynasties (Ruth 4:11–12). When Rachel, who is barren, implores her husband Jacob, "give me children" (Gen 30:1), what she really says is "build [*banah*] for me sons [*banim*]." The house (*bayith*) that God promises through the prophet Nathan to build for David (2 Sam 7:11–13) may therefore mean either the temple or his line of descendants.[4]

Oikodomein, the Greek word meaning "to build" that typically translates *banah* in the Septuagint, subsequently becomes in the New Testament a key term "for the process of the growth and the development of the community," and consequently "reflects the manifoldness of the primitive Christian understanding of the Church."[5] God is bringing forth the Church in the image of his Son, and inasmuch as the Church is being formed in Christ's image, she is being built up "in him" (Eph 2:19–22). As an early North African bishop[6] writes, "The spiritual building up of the body of Christ is brought about by love."[7] This "building up," he continues, "is never carried on more purposefully than when the Church (which is itself Christ's body) offers his body and blood under the signs of bread and wine."

---

3. Wagner, "*Banah*," 168, 175.
4. Wagner, "*Banah*," 176–77.
5. Michel, "*Oikos*," 140–41.
6. St. Fulgentius of Ruspe.
7. Kenneth, *From the Fathers*, 312.

We may even say that it is the very nature of love to build. St. Paul makes this point clearly to the Corinthians. While mere knowledge tends to puff up (*physioein*) those who lay claim to it, love, says Paul, builds up (*oikodomein*, 1 Cor 8:1). The word he uses is the same as that employed in the Septuagint for the building of the rib taken from Adam's side into a woman for him. This is divine love in action. God loves the man and does not want him to be solitary. "It is not good that the man should be alone," he says (Gen 2:18). God wills man's good—the very essence of love, according to the traditional definition of the Church[8]—so he provides him with "a helper fit for him."

God the Father's love for his Son does no less, and is evidenced in his building of the Church to be his spouse. To that end, St. Peter testifies that God's people, "like living stones, are being built up [*oikodomeisthe*] as a spiritual house [*oikos*]" (1 Pet 2:5). St. Paul puts it this way (note the frequency of derivatives of *oikos* and compounds of *oikodomein*): "You are fellow citizens with the saints and members of the household [*oikeioi*] of God, built [*epoikodomethentes*] on the foundation of the apostles and prophets, Christ Jesus himself being the cornerstone, in whom the whole structure [*oikodome*], being joined together, grows into a holy temple in the Lord. In him you also are being built together [*synoikodomeisthe*] into a dwelling place [*katoiketerion*] for God by the Spirit" (Eph 2:22–23).

While it is indeed true that this Church is built not so much by as of his people—who are, as St. Peter says, living stones—they are by no means merely passive objects of God's building activity. The very purpose of pastors and teachers within the Church, for instance, is to "equip the saints for the work of ministry, for building up [*eis oikodomein*] the body of Christ" (Eph 4:12). If we live by the truth and in love, St. Paul writes, we shall "grow up in every way" into Christ (Eph 4:15). Thus the body grows so that it "builds itself up [*eis oikodomein heautou*] in love" (Eph 4:16). By "building [our]selves up [*epoikodomein heautous*] in [our] most holy faith" (Jude 20), we participate in the Church's great vocation to be formed in Christ's image.

That this process involves growing pains on the part of the gestating Church should come as no surprise. Comprised as she is by sinners who, though redeemed, are being led on the way of sanctification, she experiences—as Israel did before her—the disciplinary hand of God when she fails to live up to her high calling. "My son, do not despise the Lord's discipline or be weary of his reproof," Solomon admonished the Israelites of his day,

---

8. Gabriel, *Divine Intimacy*, 56–7.

"for the LORD reproves him whom he loves, as a father the son in whom he delights" (Prov 3:11–12). The writer to the Hebrews invokes this passage to exhort his readers to persevere in the way of holiness:

> It is for discipline that you have to endure. God is treating you as sons. For what son is there whom his father does not discipline? If you are left without discipline, in which all have participated, then you are illegitimate children and not sons. Besides this, we have had earthly fathers who disciplined us and we respected them. Shall we not much more be subject to the Father of spirits and live? For they disciplined us for a short time as it seemed best to them, but he disciplines us for our good, that we may share his holiness. For the moment all discipline seems painful rather than pleasant, but later it yields the peaceful fruit of righteousness to those who have been trained by it. (Heb 12:7–11)

The pains of growing within the divine womb continue for the Church until the consummation of all things, at which time she is to be delivered and brought forth as depicted in St. John's rapturous vision: "I saw the holy city, new Jerusalem, coming down out of heaven from God" (Rev 21:2). The pangs of being born will be forgotten, because God "will wipe away every tear from their eyes, and death shall be no more, neither shall there be mourning, nor crying, not pain anymore, for the former things have passed away" (Rev 21:4).

The Church's Anticipatory Birth at Pentecost

While the Church grows mystically in the womb of her risen Lord, not to be brought forth until the end, she nonetheless already reaches that end in an anticipatory way when the Holy Spirit descends on the apostles at Pentecost (Acts 2:1–4).[9] The Spirit is, after all, not only the eschatological Spirit—that is, he whose coming signals the beginning of the End—but, also the Spirit of Christ (Rom 8:9), the means by which Christ returns in "a little while" (John 14:19) to his Church, well in advance of his glorious second advent. "If anyone loves me," Jesus tells his disciples in the upper room, "he will keep my word, and my Father will love him, and we will come to him and

---

9. As we will see in chapter 5, this event bears the same relation to the Church's descent from heaven in St. John's vision as do St. Stephen's vision of Jesus "standing at the right hand of God" (Acts 8:55) and St. Paul's "untimely" birth (1 Cor 15:8) when he first encounters Jesus, to Christ's second advent.

make our home with him" (John 14:23). Moreover, the very coming of the Holy Spirit is actually found to be, in the prophetic imagination, a manifestation of birth pangs—only, in this case, as loosed by the resurrection of Jesus rather than as endured by him on the cross.

In order to understand this, we need to pay careful attention to what St. Peter says to the bystanders who have witnessed the Spirit's descent. In order to explain the extraordinary event to them, he employs an extended quotation from the prophet Joel:

> In the last days it shall be, God declares, that I will pour out my Spirit on all flesh, and your sons and daughters shall prophesy, and your young men shall see visions, and your old men shall dream dreams; even on my male servants and female servants in those days I will pour out my Spirit, and they shall prophesy. And I will show wonders [*terata*] in the heavens above and signs on the earth below, blood and fire, and vapor of smoke; the sun shall be turned to darkness and the moon to blood. (Acts 2:17–20; Joel 2:28–31)

As far as the coming of the Spirit itself goes, this promise is clearly fulfilled in the ecstatic prophesying of the apostles and their companions, representing as they do what appears to be a sizable and likely diverse crowd (Acts 1:14–15). It is difficult, however, to see how the rest of the passage can be made to fit into St. Luke's description of the event. The cosmic signs—"wonders in the heavens above and signs on the earth below," "blood and fire, and vapor of smoke," "the sun turned to darkness and the moon to blood"—are nowhere in evidence on that first Pentecost of the Church. And yet it seems clear that they are somehow to be included in the Spirit's outpouring, as Joel foresees it, and as Peter understands it.

In point of fact, all these signs appear to have their background in the judgment brought against Egypt at the time of the exodus—or deliverance—of Israel from that land. It has been pointed out that, in the time of Joel, the word *mophathim* (wonders, translated by *terata* in St. Peter's sermon) was "known especially as applied to the terrible events associated with the plagues that came upon Egypt."[10] Indeed, it requires little imagination to find a correspondence between the prophetic language of Joel and the events of Exodus 7—13.

The plagues of hail (Exod 9:13–26) and of locusts[11] (Exod 10:12–20) are examples of Joel's "wonders in the heavens above," while those of frogs

---

10. Wolff, *Joel and Amos*, 68.
11. Joel's vision itself is actually described in terms of an invasion of locusts (Joel 2:25).

(Exod 8:1–7), gnats (Exod 8:16–19), flies (Exod 8:20–24), death of livestock (Exod 9:1–7), and boils (Exod 9:8–12) represent his "wonders on the earth below." By Joel's "blood" we may understand the conversion of the water of the Nile into that substance (Exod 7:14–24); by "fire," the pillar of fire (Exod 13:21b); and by "vapor of smoke," the pillar of cloud (Exod 13:21a). The plague of darkness (Exod 10:21–23), moreover, may well be the basis for the statement of Joel that "the sun" shall be "turned to darkness," and the plague of the death of the first-born (Exod 12:29–30)—which takes place during the night—may well be the source of its continuation: "and the moon to blood."

It seems highly likely, therefore, that, in the passage appropriated by St. Peter, Joel is alluding to the events leading up to and surrounding the exodus, events which Peter, by citing both the prophecy of the Spirit and the prophecy of the signs, appears to imply are renewed at the time of the Spirit's descent on the day of Pentecost. Further evidence of this connection is given in the words with which the part of Joel's prophecy quoted by St. Peter concludes: "And it shall come to pass that everyone who calls on the name of the Lord shall be saved" (Joel 2:32; Acts 2:21). At the Passover in Egypt, we recall, all those who apply lamb's blood to the door-posts and lintels of their houses (Exod 12:7)—thereby in effect calling upon the name of the Lord—are spared his judgment (Exod 12:12–13). Furthermore, at the Red Sea, when the Israelites call out to the Lord (Exod 14:10), he delivers them all (Exod 14:21–31; 12:41).

If it is true, as we have maintained,[12] that the exodus was a deliverance preceded and accompanied by birth pangs, then we may surmise that the evocative prophecy of Joel points ahead to a similar deliverance, and that St. Peter has precisely this deliverance in mind when he appropriates Joel's language in explanation of the startling outpouring of the Spirit on Pentecost. In that case, the birth in view is, of course, no longer the birth of Israel, with which we have associated the miraculous departure from Egypt. Rather, it is now associated with the complex of events that begins with the Passion and death of Jesus and reaches its culmination in the descent of the Spirit. In other words, it represents the realization or actualization, through Jesus's resurrection, of the Church's emergence into the world. The strong east wind that drives the sea back and makes it dry land for the Israelites to pass over (Exod 14:21–22) has as its natural counterpart the mighty rushing wind that the crowd hears at Pentecost

---

12. See chapter 1.

(Acts 2:2). The same Holy Spirit who hovers over the face of the waters to facilitate creation (Gen 1:2) is their common source.

Just as the Church is brought to birth through the pangs of Jesus's Passion, so—in analogy with a child newly drawn from the womb—might we say that she draws her first breath when, after his resurrection, the Spirit descends on the apostles at Pentecost, animating the new humanity superseding that which came into existence originally when "God formed the man of dust from the ground and breathed into his nostrils the breath of life, and the man became a living creature" (Gen 2:7).

This new humanity is none other than the flowering of that which is adumbrated in the new community constituted by Mary and John as they stand in the shadow of the cross. It is further instantiated in the gathering together of the eleven disciples in the upper room where Jesus appears to them after rising from the dead (Luke 24:36), and it finds its full fleshing out in that same upper room after his ascension into heaven (Acts 1:12–13), when Mary, John, and the other ten apostles are joined by the women and the brothers of Jesus (Acts 1:14), the whole company of persons eventually swelling to "in all about 120" (Acts 1:15). The climactic selection of Matthias formalizes the apostolic college (Acts 1:26) and thereby completes the core of the "one, holy, catholic and apostolic Church."

This Church's rapid growth and spread is accompanied by the pangs of persecution. The apostles are arrested and imprisoned on two occasions (Acts 4:3; 5:18), threatened with death (Acts 5:33), and beaten (Acts 5:40), but like the woman in Jesus's analogy who has sorrow while giving birth (John 16:21), their sorrow is turned into joy that they are counted worthy to suffer for Jesus (Acts 5:41). After describing Stephen's martyrdom, St. Luke tells us that "there arose on that day a great persecution against the church in Jerusalem" and that "they were all scattered throughout the regions of Judea and Samaria, except the apostles" (Acts 8:1). Even so, he later adds, "the Church throughout all Judea and Galilee and Samaria had peace and was being built up [*oikodomoumene*]" and multiplied (Acts 9:31). So it has been and will be throughout her history. To paraphrase the second-century theologian Tertullian: "The blood of the martyrs is the seed of the Church."[13]

---

13. *Plures efficimur, quotiens metimur a vobis: semen est sanguis Christianorum*, we multiply when you reap us: the blood of Christians is seed (Tertullian, *Apologeticus*, Book 13).

Bringing Forth Christ

The Church, then, is born, or brought forth, through the birth pangs of Jesus's Passion and death, issuing in resurrection, in much the same way that Israel was born, or brought forth, through the exodus from Egypt, and that Jesus himself was born of the blessed Virgin as the outcome of the messianic woes, and ultimately through resurrection. So too, as Israel proceeded to fulfill her vocation to suffer the woes of bringing forth Messiah, and as Jesus subsequently endured the pangs of the cross to bear the Church, must the Church, in her turn, experience pregnancy and a childbirth of her own: that of the Christ at his second coming.

This childbirth, it turns out, is what we might term the complement to that of the bride "coming down out of heaven from God" in St. John the Divine's vision. In fact, in the act of being brought forth, the bride is, at the same time, giving birth, as it were, to her own bridegroom, bringing him forth from her womb fully formed, as does the "woman clothed with the sun" in that other vision of St. John (Rev 12:1–6). This is so because the formation of Christ within his Church is the *sine qua non* of his glorious return, a relation which is most clearly seen in the apparently causal connection that St. Peter draws between the two. "What sort of people ought you to be in lives of holiness and godliness," he asks his readers in his second epistle, "waiting for and hastening the coming of the day of God?" (2 Pet 3:11–12).

It is the Church's perfection in Christ's own image that in effect both induces his emergence from within her and draws him once more down out of heaven from God. He comes to meet his bride, the Church, prepared and adorned for him (Rev 21:2), and once more to declare, "This at last is bone of my bones and flesh of my flesh" (Gen 2:23). As, in the beginning, the woman comes forth from the man's side to be his wife, so, in the end, does the Church, in a manner of speaking, bring him forth to be her husband.

Here it will be helpful to attend once more to what is figuratively described as the begetting of Messiah. As we have seen,[14] the expression is found in the second psalm: "I will tell of the decree: the LORD said to me, 'You are my Son; today I have begotten you.'" (Ps 2:7). We have suggested that this "today"—interpreted for us by another psalm which says of Messiah, "from the womb of the morning, the dew of youth will be yours" (Ps 110:3)—points ultimately to the first day of creation, when God said, "Let

---

14. In chapter 1.

there be light" (Gen 1:3). If this be accepted, then the birth associated with this particular begetting is located in the eschatological revelation of Christ, the firstborn not only "of all creation" (Col 1:15) but also "from the dead" (Col 1:18), underlying "new heavens and a new earth" (Isa 65:17).[15]

The New Testament, however, expands the significance of the psalmist's "today" by applying it in different contexts. To begin with, the writer of the letter to the Hebrews associates it with the begetting of Messiah in the womb of Israel: "For to which of the angels did God ever say, 'You are my Son, today I have begotten you'? Or again, 'I will be to him a father, and he shall be to me a son'?" (Heb 1:5). The latter quotation is of words originally spoken by the Lord to the prophet Nathan about King David (2 Sam 7:14). Therefore, the ensuing birth is clearly of Jesus in Bethlehem: "when [God] brings the firstborn into the world, he says, 'Let all God's angels worship him'" (Heb 1:6). According to St. Luke, this is precisely what happens when "a multitude of the heavenly host" appears to the shepherds, saying, "Glory to God in the highest, and on earth peace among those with whom he is pleased!" (Luke 2:13–14).

On the other hand, according to a well-attested marginal reading in St. Luke's Gospel, the "today" of Messiah's begetting is also alternatively identified as the day of Jesus's baptism. "When Jesus had been baptized and was praying," Luke tells us, "the heavens were opened, and the Holy Spirit descended on him in bodily form, like a dove; and a voice came from heaven, 'You are my beloved Son; *today I have begotten you*'"[16] (Luke 3:21–22). In this case, since his baptismal begetting foreshadows his death (Luke 12:50), his being born is his resurrection, in accordance with its characterization by St. Peter as the loosing of the pangs of death (Acts 2:24).[17]

Finally, as recorded in the Acts of the Apostles, St. Paul explicitly ties the psalmist's "today" to the day when God raised Jesus from the dead, making the resurrection itself, in its turn, a begetting. "We bring you the good news that what God promised to the fathers," he says, "this he has fulfilled to us their children by raising Jesus, as also it is written in the second psalm, 'You are my Son, today I have begotten you'" (Acts 13:33–34). This likewise implicitly shifts the time of birth to his eventual coming

---

15. A subject to which we will return in chapter 5.

16. Italics denote the alternative words to the reading in the canonical text ("with you I am well pleased").

17. See chapter 2.

forth at the time of the consummation of all things from the womb of the Church, which is our present focus.

From this point of view, the coming of the Holy Spirit at Pentecost—as the crowning event of the resurrection, ascension, and exaltation of Christ—represents for the Church what the annunciation is for the blessed Virgin: a moment not of birth, but of conception, or impregnation. In order that Mary may "conceive in [her] womb and bear a son" (Luke 1:31), the Holy Spirit, she is told, will come upon her and "the power of the Most High" will overshadow her (Luke 1:35). In like manner, St. Luke tells us that, when the apostles and their companions were all together in one place, "there came from heaven a sound like a mighty rushing wind," which "filled the entire house where they were sitting," and "divided tongues as of fire appeared to them and rested on each one of them" (Acts 2:1–3).

Here we have the source and the beginning of the mystery that St. Paul, writing to the Colossians, calls "Christ in you, the hope of glory" (Col 1:27). "The Church," says Yves Congar, "is a gathering of men among other gatherings of men, but bearing amongst them the mystery of Jesus Christ. She is the company of witnesses to him. Inasmuch as it depends on men's faithfulness, she brings Christ to the world, offering it opportunities to recognize him as the key to its destiny."[18]

We have already observed[19] that, speaking with his disciples on the Mount of Olives, Jesus employed the expression "the beginning of the birth pains" (Matt 24:8) in the tradition of the messianic woes. Now we can go on to say that, in doing so, he was indicating that the same process that found its end in his first advent must—with his death and resurrection, and the coming of the Holy Spirit—begin again. This is so that, as the birth pangs experienced by Israel bring forth Jesus—Messiah in lowliness and humility—those endured by the Church might bring forth the Christ—the same Messiah, in glory and honor.

It is widely recognized that the whole idea of *thlipsis* (great suffering or tribulation), as it is described in the eschatological discourses of Jesus in the synoptic Gospels (Matt 24:21; Mark 13:19; Luke 21:23[20]), as well as in the writings of St. Paul (1 Thess 5:3; 2 Tim:3.1) and in the book of Revelation (Rev 7:14), is not to be referred exclusively to some distant future and restricted in duration to a pre-determined period, or even generalized as

---

18. Congar, *Wide World My Parish*, 19.
19. See chapter 1.
20. St. Luke substitutes *anagke* (distress, calamity) for *thlipsis*.

merely afflicting the world in general, but that it has primary application to the present life and experience of the Church.[21]

The earthquakes, floods, plagues, famines, wars, and droughts so terrifyingly described in apocalyptic writings, therefore, are not in themselves correlates of the Church's sufferings but are rather symbolic manifestations of divine judgment throughout history on the secular powers who oppose Christ and his Church. It is those powers' persecution of God's people that represents the real tribulation, which in turn constitutes the birth pangs that the Church must undergo in order first to manifest and finally to bring forth the Christ into the world.

In a way somewhat analogous to that in which it is said that God himself shares in the travail of his people Israel in Egypt—"I know their sufferings," he tells Moses (Exod 3:7)—the risen Christ himself participates in the sufferings of his people, the Church, the body of which he has been constituted the head (Eph 1:22–23). As birth pangs, these sufferings recapitulate those of Israel in a general way, and yet they remain distinctive.

As we have said,[22] the messianic descent, running as it did in a direct line from one woman (Eve) to another (Mary), gave a vertical thrust to Israel's sufferings in their capacity as collective birth pangs which issued in the birth of Jesus. The birth pangs that Jesus himself suffered, however, and in particular his death and resurrection, have, in a manner of speaking, once more reoriented the suffering of God's people—now constituted as the Church—in line with their particular vocation, which is to bring forth the Christ. The Church is to be fruitful, multiply, and fill the earth (Gen 1:28) so as to lend Christ, who is its head, the anatomy of a body, and thereby once more bring him into the world. As Oscar Cullmann has said, "the Church must be a human fellowship in which Christ, the one, is 'formed'... in which he becomes incarnate."[23] To this end, we may say that, through the Church, there has been a return to the original horizontal thrust of generation and propagation by means of birth pangs.

According to St. Paul, after all, the Church itself not only has but is, in a sense, a womb. The apostle acknowledges that both he and his readers serve in that capacity in a metaphorical way when he writes to the Galatians, "I am again in the anguish of childbirth, until Christ is formed in

---

21. Allison, *End of the Ages*, 25.
22. See introduction.
23. Cullmann, *Early Church*, 130.

you!" (Gal 4:19).[24] As Edward Schillebeeckx has observed, "that which was brought to realization under the providence of the Father in the exemplar or prototype, the man Jesus"—for our purposes, his gestation and birth through his people Israel—"must now be renewed in the reproduction or antitype, the messianic family of the Church."[25]

It is noteworthy that, in St. John's eschatological vision of "the holy city, new Jerusalem, coming down out of heaven from God" (Rev 21:2), which constitutes the fulfillment of St. Paul's betrothal of her to Christ (2 Cor 11:2), the bridegroom does not immediately appear to meet her. That is because, like Eve, who reproduced her husband Adam by "getting a man with the help of the Lord" (Gen 4:1), the Church must now, through the pangs of birth that characterize her whole history, bring forth Jesus, the Christ. "Behold," he himself says—and here we may once more picture him speaking to us as though from her womb—"I am coming soon" (Rev 22:7), to which the Spirit and the Bride reply, "Come" (Rev 22:12). "Surely I am coming soon," he says (Rev 22:17). "Amen," we all affirm, "'Come, Lord Jesus!'" (Rev 22:20).

---

24. For a case study of the formation of Christ within his Church, based on the encounter between Jesus and the woman at the well in Samaria as narrated in the fourth chapter of St. John's Gospel, see appendix 1.

25. Schillebeeckx, *Christ the Sacrament*, 47.

Chapter 4

The Birth Pangs of the Christian

> My little children, for whom I am again in the anguish of childbirth until Christ is formed in you! *Galatians 4:19*

"IN OUR COMING INTO this world out of our mother's womb," says John Donne in one of his sermons, "we do not make account that a child comes right, except it come with the head forward, and thereby prefigure that headlong falling into calamities which it must suffer after."[1]

We have seen in the preceding chapter how the Church, considered as an entity otherwise known as the body of Christ, is both born from the birth pangs of Jesus and the bearer of Jesus through its own birth pangs. This fits the pattern that we have observed in the role not only of Israel (chapter 1), suffering the pains of her own delivery in the exodus from Egypt and subsequently bearing her own redeemer through the messianic woes, but also of Jesus himself (chapter 2), born initially as a result of those woes before being re-born in the Resurrection, and in turn giving birth to the Church on the cross.

Our focus now turns to the role of individual Christians who make up the Church, of whom St. Paul says that they are, on the one hand, "the body of Christ," and on the other, "individually members of it" (1 Cor 12:27). When we do so, we ought not to be surprised to find that the same pattern holds: each of us both is brought to birth through Jesus and gives birth to him. In the former case, the pangs are those that he has graciously

---

1. Kenneth, *From the Fathers*, 118.

undergone on our behalf, credited to us in our baptism (Rom 6:3–4), but in the latter, they are our own—suffered, however, equally graciously, in fellowship with him. Moreover, what we find when we look closely at the two processes is that, rather than being sequential, they are, in fact—as is the case with the Church—parallel and coterminous.

Our Being Birthed

According to the New Testament, the coming forth of new life in the spiritual sense takes place in a way analogous to the process by which human beings are conceived and gestated. It is true that the two processes are different orders of things. "That which is born of the flesh is flesh," says Jesus, "and that which is born of the Spirit is spirit" (John 3:6). And yet, as one commentator has observed, while "the one does not and cannot overflow into the other," still, "the analogy between them is so close that the natural and visible process of generation is itself the means by which the second and spiritual order is apprehended and believed in."[2]

Another writer describes the spiritual in terms of the physical as follows: "God first plants within our heart what we might call the ovum of saving faith . . . Second, he sends forth the seed of his word, which contains the divine life within it, to pierce the ovum of faith. The result is conception. Thus, a new spiritual life comes into being, a life that has its origin in God."[3] To carry the comparison to its natural conclusion, this life must grow and develop in uncomfortable ways, and its emergence from the womb is attended by the birth pains putatively undergone by the one being born.

The classic passage on spiritual birth is, of course, the record of the conversation between Jesus and Nicodemus in the third chapter of St. John's Gospel. In order better to understand the analogic relationship between physical birth pangs and their spiritual equivalent, let us look more closely at the sequence of events involved in the process of being born, using the remarks made by Jesus to Nicodemus as a guide and touchstone.

In those remarks, Jesus speaks of spiritual birth as a being "born again" or "born from above"[4] (John 3:3). Hearing from him of the necessity of such a birth, Nicodemus is thoroughly confounded. "How can

---

2. Hoskyns, *Fourth Gospel*, 215.
3. Boice, *Foundations of the Christian Faith*, 407.
4. The Greek word *anothen* is capable of either translation.

a man be born when he is old?" he asks incredulously. "Can he enter a second time into his mother's womb and be born?" (John 3:4). Jesus does not answer him directly, in part because in its literal sense the latter question is obviously absurd, and in part because it is probably intended rhetorically by Nicodemus. But in spite of this, there may be some truth in what the question implies: perhaps, in other words, there is a sense in which a person who is born again or from above does enter once more into a womb, though not the original one.

The legendary sufferer Job's first words upon realizing the full extent of the devastation that came upon him and his family sheds light on this. Indeed, it is possible that Nicodemus even had them in mind. "Naked I came from my mother's womb," Job says, "and naked shall I return" (Job 1:21). Job came forth from the woman who bore him, but he would return to another "mother," the earth. "A hard lot has been created for human beings," says one deuterocanonical author, "a heavy yoke lies on the children of Adam from the day they come out of their mother's womb, till the day they return to the mother of them all" (Sir 40:1[5]). In these terms, in order to be fully born a person must indeed first, in Nicodemus's formulation, "enter a second time into his mother's womb"—that is, die and be buried in the earth—and emerge again. In its fullest sense, then, to be born signifies the entire process initiated when life is conceived and completed when that life is finally brought forth at the moment of the resulting delivery.

The language used by Jesus to explain this mysterious new birth to Nicodemus may be understood as reflecting precisely such a process. We notice that not once, but twice, he tells him that he must experience this birth: first, in order that he may see (*idein*) the kingdom of God (John 3:3), and second, in order that he may enter (*eiselthein*) that kingdom (John 3:5). Now, it is apparent that seeing and entering are not merely interchangeable synonyms describing an identical consequence of being born. For one thing, seeing is associated with being born from above or again, whereas entering is tied to being born "of water and the Spirit." The two stand in an organic relation that may best be explicated in terms of initial conception and final delivery.

According to this interpretation, Jesus's language refers simultaneously to both conception and delivery, with first the one—the birth that precedes seeing, and that may therefore be likened to conception—and then the other—the birth that precedes entering, and that therefore may be likened

---

5. New Jerusalem Bible translation.

to delivery—being primarily in view. Because of the organic nature of their relationship, the process that they serve to initiate and conclude, respectively, has been telescoped in such a way that being conceived and being delivered appear to be one and the same thing, when in fact the two events are separated by a period of development analogous to the nine months of embryonic and fetal formation, or gestation, in the womb.

Thus we have a fresh metaphor for spiritual maturation: growth *in utero*. There are several advantages of this way of conceptualizing the Christian life. First of all, by thinking along these lines we are able to make quite clear that the new creation of which St. Paul speaks in his second letter to the Corinthians is just that: a new creation, and not one that has been merely done over or renovated. Because it is initiated by a conception, this birth is a radically new beginning: "the old has passed away," indeed, and "the new has come" (2 Cor 5:17).

Second, such a metaphor puts the dependence in our new relationship squarely where it belongs: on God. After all, in whose womb are we found but in his? "In him we live and move and have our being," St. Paul tells the Athenians, "for we are indeed his offspring" (Acts 17:28). In our status as "fetuses," we are utterly dependent on him for all things, and cannot possibly exist apart from him.[6]

Finally, this analogy opens the way toward a perspective on the Christian life that not only views the whole of that life as being in the same dependent, protected relation to God that a fetus enjoys with respect to its mother, but also—and more importantly for our purposes—enables us to identify our sufferings as the birth pains that they are.

In western tradition, it is commonly held that the water spoken of by Jesus in his conversation with Nicodemus is a reference to baptism, in which the Spirit is believed to regenerate the one baptized. According to the Church, "The symbolism of water signifies the Holy Spirit's action in baptism, since after the invocation of the Holy Spirit it becomes the efficacious sacramental sign of new birth."[7] But the same dogmatic definition goes on immediately to draw an analogy with the physical process: "Just as the gestation of our first birth took place in water, so the water of baptism truly signifies that our birth into the divine life is given to us in the Holy Spirit."

---

6. This is not to suggest that we are not utterly dependent on him before our conception, or that, at birth, we will somehow become independent and able to exist on our own. Like other metaphors, this one may be valid in what it asserts, but not necessarily in everything that it implies.

7. *Catechism of the Catholic Church*, 183.

If, therefore, Jesus's words in John 3:5 are to be understood as a response to Nicodemus's query about re-entering the womb, then, according to one writer, the water he speaks of must also have something to do with birth or coming forth from the womb:

> In ancient Near Eastern literature the word "water" can be and is used as a *terminus technicus*, or at least a well-known circumlocution, for matters involving procreation, child-bearing, child-bearing capacity, or the act of giving birth itself. Sometimes water is a circumlocution for semen, for amniotic fluid, or for the process of birth itself from the breaking of the waters to the actual delivery. In Old Babylonian, for instance, the amniotic fluid is called "water of bearing," or simply "water" (4 Esd 8:8).[8]

The same writer, moreover, calls attention to the fact that the Hebrew consonant cluster *h-y-l*, which in its verbal form is usually translated "to give birth," literally denotes "the rupturing of the amniotic sack or membrane." This writer concludes that there is little doubt that a reference to "being born of water" can be interpreted to mean "physical birth which ensues after a woman's 'waters' break,"[9] and that "the 'water' [St. John] has Jesus speak of must have something to do with birth or coming forth from the womb."[10]

The Church fathers often bring the water of baptism and the water of birth together. Following St. Cyril of Jerusalem, for instance, St. John Chrysostom "compares the water of baptism to the womb in which the embryo is formed . . . The water is used and made the means of birth to him who is born; what the womb is to the embryo, water is to the believer."[11]

Another modern observer concurs, finding a parallel to "being born through water" in Jesus's subsequent statement that "that which is born of the flesh is flesh, and that which is born of the Spirit is spirit" (John 3:6). "The experience of the breaking of water in natural birth," she writes, "makes sense of the double expression 'of water and Spirit' as a description of birth and rebirth. As always in the fourth Gospel, the experience of natural existence is interpreted in terms of a doctrine of creation: the creator

---

8. Witherington, "Waters of Birth,"156.
9. Witherington, "Waters of Birth," 158.
10. Witherington, "Waters of Birth," 156.
11. Leeming, *Principles of Sacramental Theology*, 48–49.

God creates and sustains his creation, and natural birth points beyond itself to the life which comes from God."[12]

On this interpretation, being born "of water" and being born "of the Spirit" are not only not simultaneous—as they are generally thought to be when water is equated solely with baptism—but are actually contrasted with each other, in much the same way that flesh (human nature) and spirit are contrasted by Jesus. Nevertheless, there appears at the same time to be a fundamental parallelism between them. Rather than merely serving as a prerequisite for spiritual birth—surely Jesus meant to say more than that—the physical process of being born actually provides the analogy for the spiritual birthing process.

Both begin with a conception, which in the latter is a being born from above that results in the seeing, or apprehension, of the kingdom of God. Likewise, each proceeds through an extended period of growth and development—a necessary time of gestation, with all its attendant discomfort. In the physical realm, this takes place in the watery environment of the womb, the spiritual analogue of which is the enveloping presence and pervasive influence of the Spirit. To be born, at last, is to undergo the sufferings that are necessary in order to enter the kingdom in a decisive way upon departure from this life.

Entry into the kingdom of God, therefore, does not follow immediately on being born of water and the Spirit. Jesus's words merely make the first conditional on the second. It is as though he is saying that no one born of water can enter the kingdom of God without being born of the Spirit. Having been conceived and enabled to perceive the kingdom of God, the believer must be gestated like a fetus in a womb before being delivered, as it were, into that kingdom. This is clearly St. Paul's assumption when he says to the new converts on one of his missionary journeys, "through many tribulations we must enter the kingdom of God" (Acts 14:22). Such an entry necessarily remains a future prospect, even for those who have, no doubt, previously undergone the rite of baptism.[13]

The implication of Nicodemus's question now makes sense. To enter the kingdom decisively is to die a physical death "in the Lord" (Rev 14:13) and return to that other mother, earth, from which the human race was originally

---

12. Pamment, "John 3:5," 190.

13. The fact that the wording attributed to Jesus in John 3:5 (*eiselthein eis ten basileian tou theou*) is identical to that attributed by St. Luke to Paul suggests that Jesus too has in mind a future entrance.

taken. Ironically, that death becomes the moment of actual birth, the final act in a process which begins with conception (conversion, or coming to faith) and continues in earnest at baptism. Being born spiritually can thus be represented as on a continuum from conversion (conception) through baptism (analogous in a normative sense to the quickening of the fetus in the womb) to physical death. Seen in this way, the end of our earthly life is in fact another new beginning, our birth into the kingdom.

This, of course, is the way the Church has always thought of the death of her martyrs, whose festivals commemorating the occasion of their martyrdom are customarily referred to as their birthdays (*natalitia*). As John Donne observes, "the days of the martyrs, which for our example are celebrated in the Christian Church, [are] ordinarily called the birth-day of the martyrs, yet that is not intended of their birth in this world but of their birth in the next, when by death their souls were new delivered of their prisons here, and they newly born into the kingdom of heaven. That day, upon that reason, the day of their death, was called their birth-day and celebrated in the Church by that name."[14] "The pangs of a new birth are upon me," writes St. Ignatius of his impending martyrdom.[15] If this is true, then it follows that the sufferings associated with the shedding of blood by which the martyrs are sanctified are related to their being born in such a way as to make them birth pangs.

The whole of our lives as Christians, then, is lived out, metaphorically, *in utero divino*, within the divine womb, in which we are carried and by which we are nourished and protected. As St. Paul says, "your life is hidden with Christ in God" (Col 3:3). Jesus himself alludes to this when he exhorts his disciples to "abide in me" (John 15:4). The growing, developing fetus is hidden within its mother and does not become apparent even to itself until after birth. So St. John writes to his beloved friends in Christ: "we are God's children now, and what we will be has not yet appeared" (1 John 3:2).

It is unavoidable that the birth pangs we experience in growing and finally being thrust from this protective environment should occasion pains for Jesus himself, in his role as our mother. On the one hand, he anticipates these during his earthly life in his interactions with those around him. "O faithless generation," he exclaims at one point, clearly suffering in exasperation, "how long am I to be with you? How long am I to bear with

---

14. Kenneth, *From the Fathers*, 118.
15. Ignatius, "Epistle to the Romans," 151.

you?" (Mark 9:19). As we have remarked previously,[16] Jesus is frequently said to be literally "wrenched in the gut" (*splagchnistheis*), remarkably like a woman in travail, by the needs and sufferings that he encounters in those around him. On the other hand, he feels, in an anticipatory way, precisely in the pangs of his own death on the cross, the pain of our delivery at the time of our death. When St. Paul describes himself as being "in the anguish of childbirth" (Gal 4:19), he is identifying with these very compassions (*splagchna*) of Christ. "God is my witness," he writes to the Philippians, "how I yearn for you all with the affection [*splagchna*] of Christ Jesus" (Phil 1:8).

Our Giving Birth

Having said this, we must nevertheless acknowledge that the metaphor of life *in utero*, when stated in this form, is not sufficient by itself to give either a fair, balanced, and complete view of the Christian life, or an adequate accounting of our birth pangs. A fetus may be wholly dependent on another being (its mother) for its life, but as such it also has an exclusively passive existence, that is, it is always being acted upon rather than acting. The Christian, on the other hand, also exists by acting and suffering, so that the fact that he or she is a Christian becomes known to those whom he encounters by what he does, how she suffers. He lives and suffers in the world in a certain way, acting upon it even as she is being acted upon by God. We are in full agreement, therefore, with E. L. Mascall when he insists that "what a being is precedes what it does," but we hesitate to draw from this the one-sided conclusion that "the Christian should be defined not in terms of what he himself does, but of what God has made him to be."[17]

The inadequacy of the metaphor results from the fact that it enables us to illustrate only God's acting upon us, which has—and deserves—priority but nonetheless does not convey the full picture of what it means to live and suffer as a Christian. Completeness and balance are achieved only when we also invert the metaphor, so that in addition to our existing, as it were, in the womb of God, God himself dwells *in utero* within us in the form of Christ, who has been conceived there by the Spirit and is being formed in us ultimately to be brought forth through us.[18] Just as

---

16. See chapter 2.
17. Mascall, *Christ, the Christian, and the Church*, 77.
18. St. Bonaventure's *Bringing Forth Christ: Five Feasts of the Child Jesus*, excerpts

Jesus invites us, "abide in me" (John 15:4), so does he promise—"and I in you"—to abide in us.

The growth of Jesus in us of itself engenders birth pangs for us, his blessed increase being the cause and occasion of our painful decrease, to borrow language from John the baptizer (John 3:30). As we have all caused our mothers pain by being brought into the world, quite apart from any culpable intention on our part, so is Jesus's gestation within us, of the nature of things, the occasion of much of our pain as Christians. But when God remakes us in his image, says one writer, he implants in us a "primeval urge," with the result that "deep within us is an unquenchable hunger to surround, enfold, possess, hold, embrace, as a mother does her child in her womb, God's very own life-giving Word. From that inner possession of God's life we give birth to Jesus Christ in the events of our daily lives."[19]

St. Paul expresses the same attitude when he speaks of "always carrying in the body the death of Jesus" (2 Cor 4:10a). It is striking that he couches his teaching on this subject in language that is strongly reminiscent of pregnancy. To carry the death of Jesus in the body evokes the way a pregnant woman carries her unborn child in her womb. Moreover, Paul does not use here the usual word for death (*thanatos*), but one which means literally a "putting to death" (*nekrosis*). He thus appears to intend, not just the fact of death but the manner of it—that is, in Jesus's case, crucifixion, which was, as we have seen,[20] birth pangs for him. It goes without saying, then, that this involves travail for us as those who have been—and are even now being—"crucified with Christ" (Gal 2:20).[21]

The direct consequence of carrying the death of Jesus is "that the life of Jesus may also be manifested in our bodies" (2 Cor 4:10b). In the teaching of Jesus, his death could not be separated from his resurrection. He himself never spoke of the one in isolation from the other (Mark 8:31; 9:31; 10:34). Therefore, to carry his death is also necessarily to carry his resurrection. "If we have been united in him in a death like his," St. Paul writes,

---

from which are given in appendix 3, is an elaboration of this idea. For a more contemporary application, see Wright, "Birthing Jesus," 23–44, and the synopsis of her Salesian model found in appendix 2.

19. Maloney, *Mary: The Womb of God*, 11.

20. In chapter 2.

21. It is instructive to note that St. Paul also uses the word *nekrosis* for the barrenness of Sarah's womb in Romans 4:19, prior to her miraculous bearing of Isaac, suggesting that the transformation of death into life through the cross is analogous to the transformation of a barren womb into a fruitful one.

"we shall certainly be united with him in a resurrection like his" (Rom 6:5). This comes about through the sharing of the sufferings of Jesus. "I count everything as loss because of the surpassing worth of knowing Christ Jesus my Lord," Paul says, and goes on, "For his sake I have suffered the loss of all things and count them as rubbish, in order that I may gain Christ, . . . that I may know him and the power of his resurrection, and may share his sufferings, becoming like him in his death" (Phil 3:8, 10).

Sharing in the sufferings of Christ is considered not so much as what St. Paul suffers for Christ's sake, but as what Christ is suffering with Paul for his sake, and for the sake of all his people. As one observer has said, it "means more than the mystical self-identification with the suffering Christ; it involves the thought that the sufferings endured in his own person by the apostle (who here becomes the representative type of the Christian believer) are all of a part with the sufferings which Christ endured, [so that] Christ makes himself one with the sufferer, [and] so that our sufferings become his sufferings."[22] Since, as we have maintained, the sufferings leading to his death are birth pangs, our taking part in those sufferings is a sharing in those birth pangs, and therefore in their product, resurrection life.

We might even go so far as to say that to "take up [your] cross and follow [Jesus]" (Luke 9:23) is, in one way of apprehending it, to "have this mind among yourselves, which is yours in Christ Jesus" (Phil 2:5). That is, to bear the cross in following Jesus is nothing more or less than to understand that our sufferings are birth pangs; to know that "unless a grain of wheat falls into the earth and dies, it remains alone, but if it dies, it bears much fruit" (John 12:24); to comprehend that "when a woman is giving birth, she has sorrow because her hour has come, but when she has delivered the baby, she no longer remembers the anguish, for joy that a human being has been born into the world" (John 16:21); and to realize that we "carry in the body the death of Jesus, so that the life of Jesus may also be manifested in our bodies" (2 Cor 4:10).

Understanding our sufferings as birth pangs, moreover, helps to orient our attention away from our immediate discomfort to a longed-for outcome, and in so doing, makes those sufferings more bearable. "Christ in us" is indeed—in this vale of tears where we pass our earthly lives—"our hope of glory" (Col 1:27).

It is significant in this connection that St. Paul, writing to the Philippians about his own efforts to follow Jesus, makes mention of "the power

---

22. Beare, *Commentary on Philippians*, 123–24.

of [Jesus's] resurrection" prior to the "sharing of his sufferings" (Phil 3:10). He follows this order because, in our case, the power that is available in the resurrection of Christ is necessary to make possible the enduring of—not to mention the sharing in—his sufferings. This does not, however, mean that resurrection is not the end result of suffering and death for us as well as for Jesus. Paul makes that quite clear when he goes on to say that, as he is "becoming like him in his death," he is also striving toward the goal of "the resurrection from the dead" (Phil 3:11).

On this basis alone can St. Paul make the statement that we quoted earlier from his letter to the Colossians: "I rejoice in my sufferings for your sake, and in my flesh I am filling up what is lacking in Christ's afflictions for the sake of his body, that is, the Church" (Col 1:24). As one writer has suggested, Paul here is drawing from the Jewish background of the "birth pangs of the Messiah," that is, the sufferings of God's people "as a prelude to the end-time which will herald the coming of an anointed ruler." "God sets a limit to these sufferings," he writes, "and prescribes a definite measure for the afflictions which the righteous and the Jewish martyrs are required to endure (1 Enoch 47). Paul takes over this notion and bends it to his purpose. In his life of service to the Gentile churches he is called upon to represent his people as a martyr figure and to perform a vicarious ministry (2 Cor 1:6), and in this way he completes the still deficient tally of sufferings which God's new Israel has to endure before the end of the age."[23]

Nonetheless, the Christian appropriation of his meaning, according to Caryll Houselander, is that, "because Christ is in us, any suffering of ours is his Passion. He took all human suffering, great and small, and wed himself to it, crowned it with his crown of thorns, clothed it in his purple garment, gave it the power of his love. Christ's Passion redeems, not because it is our pain, but because it is his love infused into our pain."[24] "By his Passion and death on the cross," says the Roman catechism, "Christ has given a new meaning to suffering: it can henceforth configure us to him and unite us with his redemptive Passion."[25] Our suffering is his, and his, ours. The same may be said, therefore, of the birth pangs that we share.

Thus, even as God is carrying us and bearing us up, so we too are carrying him and making him visible to the world through our flesh. Our actions and our sufferings are our own, as is responsibility for them. Yet,

23. Martin, *Philippians*, 70.
24. Houselander, *Passion of the Infant Christ*, 61.
25. *Catechism*, 376.

like pregnant mothers, our lives are to be increasingly influenced by the life of Christ that stirs within us, until eventually our every move is affected—and ultimately, God willing, effected—by him, and all our actions are finally determined to serve him alone.

As Houselander has said elsewhere, "if Christ is growing in us, if we are at peace, recollected, because we know that however insignificant our life seems to be, from it he is forming himself, we shall find that we are driven more and more to act on the impulse of his love."[26] "It is only necessary," she goes on,

> to give ourselves to that life [growing in us] all that we are, to pray without ceasing, not by a continual effort to concentrate our minds but by a growing awareness that Christ is being formed in our lives from what we are. We must trust him for this, because it is not a time to see his face, we must possess him secretly and in darkness, as the earth possesses the seed. We must not try to force Christ's growth in us, but with a deep gratitude for the light burning secretly in our darkness, we must fold our concentrated love upon him like earth, surrounding, nourishing, and holding the seed.

St. Paul puts it this way: "It is no longer I who live, but Christ who lives in me. And the life that I now live in the flesh I live by faith in the Son of God who loved me and gave himself for me" (Gal 2:19–20). "Paul's profound insight into the Christian experience," as revealed here, says Joseph Fitzmyer, is found in his notion of "the reshaping of man's very physical life by the transcendent influence of Christ's indwelling."[27]

This is what Dietrich Bonhoeffer calls "formation," or "conformation," which comes about "only by [our] being drawn in into the form of Jesus Christ." "It is achieved," he writes, "only when the form of Jesus Christ works upon us in such a manner that it molds our form in its own likeness. Christ remains the only giver of forms."[28] St. Augustine said much the same thing in the fifth century: "Christ is formed in a believer through faith implanted in [the] inmost soul [of] him who accepts his form; and he receives the form of Christ who cleaves to Christ with spiritual love. The result is that through this imitating he becomes, in the measure permitted to him, the same as Christ whom he imitates."[29] Indeed, this is

---

26. Houselander, *Reed of God*, 45.
27. Fitzmyer, "Letter to the Galatians," 241.
28. Bonhoeffer, *Ethics*, 80.
29. Kenneth, *From the Fathers*, 243.

precisely what we witness happening to the woman who encounters Jesus at the well in Samaria.[30]

The Christian life is truly pregnant with meaning when viewed in the twofold manner that we have attempted to set forth. That manner is analogous to the mutual indwelling of Jesus and his people: "you in me, and I in you" (John 14:20). As Christians in the world, we are always both being borne and bearing, being brought forth and bringing forth, being birthed and giving birth. But at the same time it is, in the final analysis, not we at all but Christ who is being borne, Christ who is being brought forth, Christ who is being birthed.

Even when thought of as taking place within or through us, this travail of bringing forth Christ cannot, therefore, be considered as the consequence of our work, as though it were the result of our efforts, any more than the child to whom a woman gives birth is the product of her efforts. Like her, we can only stand by and marvel at God's work within us, and the closer our proximity to it—like that of the expectant mother—the greater our sense of wonder and our certainty that, through the suffering of birth pangs, we are made participants in a miracle quite beyond any natural capacity, ability, or power of our own.

When he is told that his mother and brothers and sisters are outside seeking him, Jesus asks rhetorically, "Who are my mother and my brothers?" He then looks at those who are sitting around him and answers his own question, "Here are my mother and my brothers! For whoever does the will of God, he is my brother and sister and mother" (Mark 3:32–35).

---

30. See appendix 1.

Chapter 5

The Birth Pangs of the Cosmos

> We know that the whole creation has been groaning together in the pains of childbirth until now. *Romans 8:22*

According to St. Paul, the birth pangs experienced in turn by Israel, Jesus himself, the Church, and Christians individually are being duplicated even now by the whole universe of which we are all a part, as it labors to bring forth on a cosmic scale the new creation that traces its inception to the risen body of Christ. Not only that, but all the pains of the former are recapitulated in the travail that results in the revelation of "a new heaven and a new earth" (Rev 21:1; Isa 65:17).

In the case of the created order, the pattern that we have heretofore observed of being born and giving birth holds, but—perhaps even more than in the instances that we have previously considered—the excruciating travail of final delivery is clearly delineated from the discomfiting period of pregnancy.

The Birth of Earth and Sky

The first version of the creation account given in Genesis could not be clearer: God speaks the universe into existence. "God said" (Gen 1:3, 6, 9, 11, 14, 20, 24, 26), and "it was so." This is in marked contrast to the contemporary creation stories of Israel's neighbors, which depicted the creative act as a birthing of the world from the body of a mother goddess.

For the writers of the Pentateuch and the rest of the Old Testament, the God of Israel was most emphatically not a fertility god, bringing heaven and earth into being out of her own fecundity.

And yet, the only insight the Scriptures give us into how God speaks the universe into existence implies what appears to be a kind of birthing process for the earth itself. Alluding to "the beginning of creation," St. Peter writes in his second epistle that, while "the heavens existed long ago," "the earth was formed out of water and through water by the word of God" (2 Pet 3:4–5). Far from contradicting the dogmatic teaching of the Church that God created the universe out of nothing (*ex nihilo*),[1] Peter merely provides his readers with a more nuanced view. First of all, according to his assertion, the heavens—which are, after all, given priority in the Genesis account[2]—precede the earth and are undoubtedly made *ex nihilo*.

For its part, the earth is, in its inchoate beginning, "without form and void, and darkness was over the face of the deep" (Gen 1:2). Thus is introduced by the author of Genesis the notion of a vast sea as a kind of material source, likewise produced *ex nihilo*, prior to the speaking of the creative word of God. This is made explicit by what follows: "And the Spirit of God was hovering over the face of the waters." Here we find the basis for the biblical cosmogony of St. Peter. Out of these waters—apparently the primeval element created by God—earth and sky[3] were formed. But it is also "through" (that is, by means of) water, in Peter's characterization, that their formation takes place, and this is where we find the implication of a kind of birth—a birth brought about, as he is careful to add, "by the word of God."

If this be accepted, the question arises, does God experience birth pangs—metaphorically speaking, of course—in birthing this creation? The whole process is, after all, described quite emphatically in terms of labor for him: "Thus the heavens and the earth were finished, and all the host of them. And on the seventh day God finished his work that he had done, and he rested on the seventh day from all his work that he had done. So God blessed the seventh day and made it holy, because on it God rested from all his work that he had done in creation" (Gen 2:1–3).

---

1. *Catechism of the Catholic Church*, 78.

2. "In the beginning, God created the heavens and the earth" (Gen 1:1).

3. The "expanse" (Gen 1:6), or firmament (called "Heaven" by God, Gen 1:8), that separated the waters that were under it (that is, the Seas, Gen 1:10) from those that were above it (the heavens, Gen 1:9).

Thomas Bennett has argued persuasively that the creator does suffer like a woman in travail. Calling the act of creation "the first labor of God,"[4] Bennett cites as witness the words of the psalmist: "Before the mountains were brought forth, or ever you had formed the earth and the world, from everlasting to everlasting you are God" (Ps 90:2). "The decisive import of the labor metaphor," according to him, is that "though God is 'from age to age,' when [he] decides to give birth to the world [he] does not expect to be excused from the natural course of things: with birth come pain, struggle, and sometimes loss. God can expect to outlast the destructive forces that accompany creative enterprises, but [he] is nevertheless willing to undergo them."[5]

Behind the Genesis creation account of the earth's being "without form and void," Bennett discerns "something like malignant chaos," and suggests that "creation was an act of primordial combat through which God is pictured as subduing the chaos to goodness." He concludes that

> God creates in Genesis in a way that is analogous to the way [he] gives birth at the cross. Creation is a challenge, it incurs a cost, but it is nonetheless non-violent in that [while] coercion is present, [this is] in such a way that the results of coercion are "good." Athanasius writes, "There is thus no inconsistency between creation and salvation, for the one Father has employed the same agent for both works, effecting the salvation of the world through the same Word who made it in the beginning" (*On the Incarnation*, 1). Of course Athanasius is thinking of the creation through John 1:3, where the Logos is the agent of creation. But we are called to add that the work of the cross and the work of creation, both accomplished through the Son, bear the striking marks of the same fashioner, the same labor, the same God from age to age. Divine travails at creation and cross illuminate the connection between the two actions of the one God and also give good reason to suspect a kind of pathos internal not only to [his] acts but also to [his] being.[6]

The universe, therefore, may be said to be brought forth in a manner analogous to birth, and consequently, God himself may be said in some sense to suffer birth pangs in the process.

---

4. Bennett, *Labor of God*, 53.
5. Bennett, *Labor of God*, 55.
6. Bennett, *Labor of God*, 56–57.

Mother Earth

The demise of the dogma that the earth is the center of the cosmos began when Galileo demonstrated that, contrary to the commonsense view based on empirical observation that the sun rises and sets, what actually moves is in fact a rotating earth that revolves around the sun. Subsequent astronomical observations, of course, have dislodged the sun, as well, from its privileged position, by revealing how relatively puny even it is and how insignificant in comparison with billions of other suns in just our galaxy, which is itself but one of billions like it. In light of this, the earth is perhaps best likened to a single grain among all the sands of her own vast seashores in terms of her cosmic status.

And yet, none of this imperils in the least the biblical conviction that it is from the earth that the transformation of the entire universe will come about. Humanity, after all—unique in all the worlds that our exploration of space has so far revealed to us—was formed "of dust from the ground" (Gen 2:7), so that, as has frequently been pointed out, we are a composite of the substances from which all the stars were originally formed. Then God himself assumed our nature by becoming flesh (John 1:14) as a man named Jesus and underwent death, and his body was buried in the ground, like a mustard seed sown in a field (Matt 13:31–32). Vivified on the third day, he converted the tomb into a womb and emerged from it, himself the bodily nucleus of the promised new creation. It is by this single act that the earth itself truly becomes the "mother of us all" (Sir 40:1).

Jesus is, however, only the first-fruits (1 Cor 15:20) of the harvest that the earth will yield. As he himself says, "Unless a grain of wheat falls into the earth and dies, it remains alone, but if it dies, it bears much fruit" (John 12:24). Such, indeed, is the power of Jesus's death and resurrection that it immediately causes the earth to give up (Rev 20:13), pre-emptively, a token number of the dead who are in her. Their tombs, too, have become little wombs from which, "after [Jesus's] resurrection," "many bodies of the saints who had fallen asleep were raised" (Matt 27:52–53) in anticipation of the general resurrection at the consummation of all things.

The earth is thereby revealed to be, as it were, pregnant with the dead who have died "in the Lord" (Rev 14:13). Their bodies lie in the ground like embryos in their mother's womb, awaiting a quickening to life. Ezekiel's vision of Israel as dry bones (Ezek 37:1–2) may be extrapolated to all of humanity. What God promises to do for them is there described in terms that are remarkably like the fetal development of gestation: "I will lay sinews upon you, and will cause flesh to come upon you, and cover you with skin" (Ezek 37:6). It is but the repetition of their original formation, also couched in terms of an underground development. "You formed my inward parts," the psalmist says, "you knitted me together in my mother's womb . . . My frame was not hidden from you, when I was being made in secret, intricately woven in the depths of the earth" (Ps 139:13, 15).

This gestation of bodies in the earth is the source of the earth's birth pangs, which begin with the death and burial of Abel, whose blood cries out to God from the ground that opened its mouth to receive it from Cain's hand (Gen 4:10–11). "We know," writes St. Paul to the Romans, "that the whole creation has been groaning together in the pains of childbirth until now" (Rom 8:22). The apparent inference is that natural cataclysms function as manifestations of the earth's maternal travail, and of these perhaps no more fitting example can be found than that of the seismic quaking of the ground. Earthquakes, indeed, feature prominently in the prophetic and apocalyptic literature as features of impending judgment and signs of God's imminent intervention (Isa 2:10–12; 13:4–13; Jer 10:10; Amos 8:8–9; Nah 1:5–6; Zech 14:4–5). Their significance culminates in the shaking of the earth that bookends Jesus's death and resurrection.

The tradition preserved in St. Matthew's Gospel records the occurrence of two earthquakes in the final days of Jesus's earthly sojourn. The first takes place at the time of his death: "Jesus cried out again with a loud voice and yielded up his spirit. And behold, the curtain of the temple was torn in two, from top to bottom. And the earth shook, and the rocks were split" (Matt 27:50–52). A second earthquake attends his resurrection: "Now after the Sabbath, toward the dawn of the first day of the week, Mary Magdalene and the other Mary went to see the tomb. And behold, there was a great earthquake, for an angel of the Lord descended from heaven and came and rolled back the stone and sat on it" (Matt 28:1–2).

In the first case, as one writer has said, "Nature was expressing sympathy with the sufferings of the redeemer"[7] by undergoing birth pangs similar to those that he was experiencing. In the other—since St. Matthew is careful, in the wake of the earthquake that follows Jesus's death, to say that it is only after his resurrection that the tombs were opened and many bodies of the saints who had fallen asleep were raised—the earth is, as we have previously suggested, pre-emptively giving up her dead as a kind of childbirth.

---

7. Plummer, *Gospel according to St. Mark*, 357.

Between these two earthquakes, as it were, all the travails that constitute the earth's birth pangs may be summarily located. We are referring, in particular, to the great period of so-called "tribulation" (Rev 7:14) described in various ways throughout the book of Revelation as immediately preceding the consummation. Far from being restricted to the end times, however, the great sufferings of the earth and its inhabitants depicted therein are those that have characterized its existence from the initial time of rebellion against God's rule and reign. This may perhaps be best illustrated from the passage in the book of Revelation detailing the opening of the "seven seals" (Rev 5:1).

The first seal opened by the Lamb appropriately reveals a white horse, whose rider "had a bow, and a crown was given to him, and he came out conquering, and to conquer" (Rev 6:1–2). By this, we may say, is signified God's rule and reign over all that immediately follows. At the opening of the second seal, "out came another horse, bright red," whose rider "was permitted to take peace from the earth, so that people should slay one another, and he was given a great sword" (Rev 6:3–4). Here, then, is the rebellion begun by the disobedience of Adam and Eve, upsetting the peace of paradise, and bearing its initial fruit in the slaying of Abel by his brother Cain and the vengeance it threatened to provoke (Gen 4:15). A black horse comes next, at the third seal's opening, and "its rider had a pair of scales in his hand" (Rev 6:5–6), representing the judgment—epitomized in the form of the deluge in the time of Noah—brought upon the earth by the wickedness of its inhabitants (Gen 6:5–13).

The opening of the fourth seal inaugurates the dire consequences of this judgment. It reveals a pale horse whose "rider's name was Death" (Rev 6:7). Along with Hades, he is "given authority over a fourth of the earth, to kill with sword and with famine and with pestilence and by wild beasts of the earth" (Rev 6:8). Though doubtless exaggerated somewhat, this proportion is nonetheless a reasonable approximation of humanity's losses over the millennia due to the ravages of war, natural disaster, and predation. The opening of this seal is followed by a brief respite at the fifth seal's opening. "The souls of those who had been slain for the word of God and for the witness they had borne" through all the earth's tribulations are told to rest a little longer until their number should be complete (Rev 6:9–11).

What comes next corresponds to the cosmic shudder at the death of Jesus on the cross, expressed in hyperbolic language rooted in the events that marked his final hours: "When [the Lamb] opened the sixth seal, I [John] looked, and behold, there was a great earthquake, and the sun became black as sackcloth, the full moon became like blood, and the stars of the sky fell to the earth as the fig tree sheds its winter fruit when shaken by a gale. The sky vanished like a scroll that is being rolled up, and every mountain and island was removed from its place" (Rev 6:12–14).These convulsions are symbolic of the earth's birth pangs. Their implied association with the Lord's Passion and death necessitates a solemn interlude during which "the servants of our God" are themselves sealed (Rev 7:3) and protected from harm because, already having "come out of the great tribulation," "they have washed their robes and made them white in the blood of the Lamb" (Rev 7:14).

When the seventh seal is opened, the scene has shifted to heaven, where there is a short silence (Rev 8:1), no doubt signifying the three days and three nights that the Son of man lay in the heart of the earth between his death and resurrection (Matt 12:40). Afterward, in response to the prayers of the saints represented by the incense offered on the golden altar before the throne of God (Rev 8:3), an angel "took the censer and filled it with fire from the altar and threw it on the earth, and there were peals of thunder, rumblings, flashes of lightning," and, he adds, "an earthquake" (Rev 8:5)—this time, the one that marks Jesus's resurrection. This signifies that God's will—which Jesus taught his disciples to ask be done (Matt. 6:10)—must continue to be carried out, and that the tribulations suffered on and by the earth must therefore also continue to the end, when their character as birth pangs will be finally revealed and their function fulfilled.

New Heavens and a New Earth

It is safe to assume, we believe, that there will be some kind of continuity between the cosmos—the heavens and the earth, in biblical language, that currently exists—and what will take its place. Exactly how the transition from one to the other will be made—how, in other words, the new creation promised both by Isaiah and by St. John the Divine will be brought about in relation to the old—is nowhere set forth in the Scriptures.

St. Peter, however, once again gives us a tantalizing glimpse into the process by picturing a destruction of the old by fire to prepare the way for the new. "The heavens and earth that now exist," he writes in the continuation of the same passage that we cited previously, "are stored up for fire," by which "the heavens will be . . . dissolved, and the heavenly bodies will melt as they burn!" (2 Pet 3:7, 12). This may sound like complete destruction and even annihilation—and therefore a contradiction of God's own solemn promise, after the great flood, that he would "never again curse the ground because of man" (Gen 8:21)—but it must be read in the context of the judgment with which St. Peter is pre-occupied. Not everything, it would appear from a close reading of his words, will actually be destroyed, but only the ungodly and the works that are done on the earth, along with the heavenly bodies (2 Pet 3:10), those celestial elements which in the popular imagination represent powers that are opposed to God.

Given almost in passing, St. Peter's aforementioned description of the original creative process is perhaps even more germane to an understanding of his thinking regarding the manner of emergence of its replacement. As we have already had occasion to observe, it suggests a kind of birth, in this case out of the primordial waters over the face of which the Spirit of God was hovering in the beginning.

According to St. Peter, "the world that then existed"—that is, the world as it was before the flood that took place in Noah's time, representing God's judgment of its wickedness—"was deluged with water and perished" (2 Pet 3:6). Of course, that world as a whole did not perish. It was only purged of the unrighteousness that pervaded it. If we are justified in assuming that the protological process will be repeated in its eschatological equivalent, it would seem that the same world which we now inhabit, rather than being destroyed, will be purged "by the same word" (2 Pet 3:7) and will once more be "formed out of water and through water" (2 Pet 3:5). This, then, is the water that will, by means of travail, bring the new creation to birth out of the old, and—in the process—ultimately extinguish the fire of judgment.

"The creation waits with eager longing," says St. Paul, "for the revealing of the sons of God" (Rom 8:19), because at that time, "the creation itself will be set free from its bondage to corruption and obtain the freedom of the glory of the children of God" (Rom 8:21). To judge from the language that Paul uses to describe it, this is to happen as a kind of birth. Yves Congar has this passage in mind when he observes that, "for the New Testament, this world's history is as it were one long and agonizing bringing to birth of a new world that is to be."[8] As another writer has said,

> the eschatological redemption of the earth and man is anticipated in the protological creation of man from the earth. The *toledoth*[9]

---

8. Congar, *Wide World My Parish*, 161.

9. "Begettings," from *yalad*, to bear, bring forth, beget (Johnson, *Purpose of the Biblical Genealogies*, 14).

pattern ("this is the book of the generations," found in Gen 5:1; 6:9; 10:1; 11:10, 27), first applied to the earth bringing forth Adam (created of dust), establishes the biblical image of mother earth as a womb (Job 1:26; Ps 139:15). In Pauline theology, the eschatological consummation is expressed in terms of the travail of the earth in childbirth, the resurrection of the last day becoming the final cosmic *toledoth*, when the earth brings forth the sons of God (redeemed from dust, Rom 8:22).[10]

That these birth pangs are the metaphorical equivalent of human sufferings is made clear both by the general context of the eighth chapter of the letter to the Romans and by the parallel drawn to human experience. St. Paul's theme in this section of Romans is the suffering of God's people, particularly in its role or function as the means to glory. He introduces this theme in relation to the sufferings of Christ, which we are to share. We are, he says, "fellow heirs with Christ, provided we suffer with him in order that we may also be glorified with him" (Rom 8:17).

It is distinctly possible, according to one commentator, that in this passage St. Paul has in mind the birth pangs of Messiah.[11] Another concludes that, while it is difficult "to document what is regularly described as 'the messianic woes' for the period before Paul," nonetheless, "all the elements of it are here—inheritance (that is, coming kingdom), suffering as a necessary preliminary, and assurance of coming glory which will eclipse all the preceding anguish. Paul draws them together as a statement of conviction in [a] non-argumentative way, which suggests that he is giving voice to a well-known even if not necessarily widely-held view of the future."[12]

"I consider that the sufferings of this present time," writes St. Paul, "are not worth comparing to the glory that is to be revealed to us" (Rom 8:18). Because creation too will share that glory, it must also share in human sufferings. Therefore, even as we "groan inwardly" (Rom 8:23), so too the creation "has been groaning together" as though in the throes of childbirth (Rom 8:22). Glory is but the consequence of the loosing, or release, of those birth pangs, just as it is the consequence of the loosing of the pangs of death in the resurrection of Christ.[13] In neither case does

10. Gage, *Gospel of Genesis*, 23.
11. Black, *Romans*, 122.
12. Dunn, *Romans 1-8*, 469.
13. The word *lyein*, to loose or release, used in St. Peter's expression "loosing the pangs of death" (Acts 2:24), is not found here. St. Paul instead employs a derivative term, *apolytrosis*, to describe the redemption of our bodies (Rom 8:23). The setting free of

the language connote the act of birth itself, but in the context of "the pains of childbirth" (Rom 8:22), it suggests the same kind of release that is entailed in the bringing forth of a child from the confines of the womb, through the narrow channel of the birth canal.

The fact that "the whole creation has been groaning together in the pains of childbirth until now" indicates that nothing less than new heavens and a new earth (2 Pet 3:13) are in the process of being born out of the old. "In such a strongly eschatological context," says one writer, "the word 'now' should be given its full eschatological force" as "the 'now' of eschatological salvation in which the process of salvation is being worked out, . . . with the present labor pains giving promise of the cosmic birth of the new age."[14]

Final delivery, however, awaits full formation of Christ's body on earth—"the revealing of the sons of God" (Rom 8:19), which will coincide with the Lord's glorious second advent.

The Day of the Lord

This brings us to the tribulation (*thlipsis*) that is associated most closely with the final intervention of God in human history at the second coming of our Lord—what we might call, in birthing terms, the delivery. Upon closer examination, this *thlipsis* turns out to be characteristic of the whole period of the "last days" (Acts 2:17; 2 Tim 3:1; Heb 1:2) that extend from Jesus's resurrection and the coming of the Holy Spirit to the general resurrection at the consummation of all things. While, on the one hand, this is the full term of pregnancy for the Church, on the other, it represents for the cosmos the final agonizing pangs of birth. As Rudolph Schnackenburg has pointed out, the Greek word *thlipsis* "is used in apocalyptic literature for the distress experienced at the end of time."[15] "This is a word," Raymond Brown says,

> that is used almost technically to describe the tribulation that will precede God's eschatological action, for example, in Daniel 12:1[-2], as it is rendered in the [Septuagint: "That day will be a day of suffering [*thlipsis*], which has not been from the beginning until that day. And on that day the whole people, as many as

---

creation from its bondage to corruption (Rom 8:21) is expressed by a root form having to do with liberation (*eleutheria*).

14. Dunn, *Romans 1–8*, 473.
15. Schnackenburg, *Gospel according to St. John*, 3:158.

should be found written in the book, will be exalted, and many of those sleeping in the breadth of the earth will be raised up."[16] In Zephaniah 1:14–15 we hear: "The great day of the LORD is near . . . That day is a day of great wrath, a day of suffering [*thlipsis*], and anguish." In the New Testament *thlipsis* is used by Jesus to describe the suffering or tribulation that will precede the coming of the Son of man (Mark 13:19, 24; Rom 2:9). By a type of realized eschatology the afflictions of the Church in her time on earth come to be regarded as *thlipsis* (Mark 4:17; Acts 11:19). In harmony with the symbolism wherein the combined death and resurrection of Jesus is represented by the messianic birth of a child, St. John sees the disciples' suffering at the death of Jesus as *thlipsis* which precedes the emergence of the definitive divine dispensation [John 16:20–22].[17]

This one event was known as "the day of the LORD" (Amos 5:18). It was anticipated by the prophets at some indefinite point in the future and would, they warned, involve severe suffering. It was also pictured as a cataclysmic occurrence attended by judgment and great devastation. One writer describes its development as follows:

> The original form of the day of [the Lord] must have been one of a fateful day decreed by [God]. Therefore we may also imagine . . . that originally there were perhaps several days of [the Lord]. But during the development of Israelite history, both religious and secular, the conception of this day became more and more singularized and definitely attached to the future. Its scope was originally limited to the national interest of the Hebrews, and it was expected that the fate of the nation would be newly shaped on "that day." And by further development the original narrow nationalistic scope was enlarged into something international, global, and universal, to become finally of cosmic significance. Parallel with this spatial expansion was a change in its temporal meaning. From the day which was very near and was one from among these "coming days" and which, after it had already passed, should not definitely interrupt the course of world history, it became a final day marking the last events at the end of ages, that eternal day of the last judgment.[18]

---

16. Our own translation.
17. Brown, *Gospel according to John (XIII–XXI)*, 730.
18. Cerny, *Day of Yahweh*, 79–80.

Daniel's "son of man" (Dan 7:13), who is manifest, in his first coming, as Jesus, now awaits the formation and manifestation of the Christ within his body (the Church) as the necessary precondition for his second coming, which coincides with this day of the Lord. We advert once more to "the Bride, the wife of the Lamb" (Rev 21:9), pictured by St. John as "the holy city Jerusalem coming down out of heaven from God" (Rev 21:10). As we have suggested,[19] her descent—preceded as it is by the birth pangs of plagues and tribulations—can be likened to uterine birth, the antitype of the emergence of Eve from the side of Adam, fully formed as she is in all her glory.

Christ will come to meet her—the bridegroom taking his bride—when he recognizes himself in her, in the same way that Adam, upon whom "the LORD God caused a deep sleep to fall" (Gen 2:21) while he took one of his ribs and fashioned it into a woman, recognized her when he awoke. Like Adam, Jesus himself does not know the time when the Father will present to him his spouse. "Concerning that day or that hour," he tells his disciples, referring to the coming of the Son of man, "no one knows, not even the angels in heaven, nor the Son, but only the Father" (Mark 13:32). But when the Father brings forth the Church, we might well expect Christ's words to be like those of Adam when Eve is brought to him: "This at last is bone of my bones and flesh of my flesh" (Gen 2:23).

Just as Messiah stands at the end of earthly Israel's longing, so does the Son of man stand at the end of human and cosmic history. The account that St. Luke gives of Stephen's martyrdom in the Acts of the Apostles is illustrative of this. In a long speech delivered before the Jewish Sanhedrin, Stephen rehearses the story of the nation, beginning with God's appearance to Abraham and continuing up to the time of David. When he comes to the Jews' ill treatment of the prophets, his listeners become incensed. In the face of their opposition—the culmination, as it were, of the opposition of their ancestors to the Holy Spirit—Stephen, filled with that same Spirit, "gazed into heaven and saw the glory of God, and Jesus standing at the right hand of God" (Acts 7:55). "Behold, I see the heavens opened," he says, "and the Son of Man standing at the right hand of God" (Acts 7:56).

St. Luke's presentation of the trial of Stephen seems calculated to put this eschatological figure in place as the climax of world history, the goal toward which it is moving. Jesus stands there in glory, awaiting not only Stephen (the first martyr), but also all "the dead who die in the Lord from now

---

19. See chapter 4.

on" (Rev 14:13). And surely it is no coincidence that the resemblance of Stephen to Jesus is also accentuated by Luke. The martyr's face initially "was like the face of an angel" (Acts 6:15), and his final words (Acts 7:59–60)—"Lord, do not hold this sin against them" and "Lord Jesus, receive my spirit"—are patterned after those of Jesus on the cross (Luke 23:34; 46).

Likewise, the revelation to St. Paul—related by St. Luke almost immediately after Stephen's speech and martyrdom—gives us a glimpse of the goal to which the Church is tending. As is well known, the conversion of the apostle takes place as he is on a mission to arrest and extradite "any belonging to the Way" (Acts 9:2) for trial and punishment in Jerusalem before the Sanhedrin. On the road to Damascus, "suddenly a light from heaven flashed around him. And falling to the ground, he heard a voice saying to him, 'Saul, Saul, why are you persecuting me?' And he said, 'Who are you, Lord?' And he said, 'I am Jesus, whom you are persecuting. But rise and enter the city, and you will be told what you are to do'" (Acts 9:3-6).

With the exception of the vision given to St. Stephen and that accorded to St. John on the island of Patmos—an apocalyptic vision, which is quite different in character from what Stephen and Paul experience—this is the only instance recorded in the New Testament of an appearance of the ascended Christ. The fact that the Lord reveals himself to the apostle to inaugurate his ministry is of utmost importance for the future of the Church. Actually, St. Paul's personal encounter with Jesus serves to foreshadow the consummation of the Church's mission at the second coming of her Lord.

As we have pointed out,[20] the Church as a whole and believers individually are not only bringing forth (or giving birth to) Christ but also being brought to birth by him. St. Paul acknowledges his maternal role (and that of his readers) when he describes the Galatians as "my little children, for whom I am again in the anguish of childbirth until Christ is formed in you" (Gal 4:19). Elsewhere, however, he alludes to his own birth, as it were, in Christ. Writing to the church at Corinth, he speaks of the appearances of the Lord to his followers after the Resurrection. First, Paul says, Jesus appeared to Peter (Cephas) and to the twelve disciples as a group, then to more than five hundred of the brothers at one time, to James, and to all the apostles (1 Cor 15:5–7). "Last of all," he writes, "as to one untimely born, he appeared also to me" (1 Cor 15:8).

The striking expression, "one untimely born," is literally "an aborted fetus" (*ektroma*). As C. K. Barrett points out, the expression has a primarily

---

20. See chapters 3 and 4.

chronological significance, the sense of which, he says, is "one hurried into the world before his time."[21] The problem this raises is that "as Christian and apostle, Paul came into being not early, but later than others," and so, to Barrett, the word "seems inappropriate," an odd choice. This difficulty disappears, however, when we consider the possibility that the comparison St. Paul is making is not between himself and the other apostles who come before him to whom Christ has appeared, but those believers to whom Christ will appear after him, specifically, at his second coming.

If St. Paul is born without "the due period of gestation,"[22] this is so, not in relation to his predecessors, who accompany Jesus during his ministry, but to the Church, which has not yet attained the necessary maturity to be brought into his presence (1 Cor 3:1–4; 2 Cor 12:1–6; Eph 4:11–13). In other words, Paul is, in effect, like Shakespeare's MacDuff, "from his mother's womb untimely ripp'd,"[23] so that he might encounter the Lord. The implication is that those who come after him will have their encounter with the Son of man—that is, the Christ—when they come to a natural birth. This will happen only when the Church, as the body of Christ, is fully formed and ready to be brought forth to him. His revelation to St. Paul on the road to Damascus is therefore seen to be anticipatory of the Lord's appearance to all humanity at his glorious second coming.

The Coming Forth of Christ

What we have said so far suggesting a seemingly gradual coming of our Lord may seem to contradict the clear teaching of Scripture that his advent will be sudden and precipitous. Jesus does, after all, tell his disciples that "as the lightning comes from the east and shines as far as the west, so will be the coming of the Son of Man" (Matt 24:27). Heretofore, we have maintained that a process is involved, one only perhaps slightly less lengthy than that which was entailed in his first advent. However, if we consider that initial coming actually to have its beginning not at his birth, but at the creation of the world when "the light of the world" (John 8:12) enters the darkness, we see that it too was a process, culminating in the personal appearance of the Word as man. On this analogy, the second

---

21. Barrett, *Commentary on First Corinthians*, 344.
22. Barrett, *Commentary on First Corinthians*, 344.
23. *The Tragedy of Macbeth*.

coming may be said to begin with the resurrection of Christ and end with his personal appearance as Son of man.

Meanwhile, the work of forming his body into his image must be accomplished. Because the latter is also his bride (2 Cor 11:2; Rev 19:7–8; 21:2; 22:17), Christ must wait until she is prepared for him. The pattern for this has already been established in the story of the first man, Adam, to whom St. Paul points us when, in the context of a long passage on the Resurrection, he draws a comparison with Christ. "The first man Adam became a living being," writes the apostle, alluding to Genesis 2:7, and "the last Adam became a life-giving Spirit" (1 Cor 15:45). The latter appears to be an allusion to the Spirit of Christ by whom life is given to his dead body in resurrection (Rom 8:9, 11) and the Church brought to birth at Pentecost. The resulting "spiritual body" comes only after the "natural body," because—as "the first man was from the earth, a man of dust"— "the second man is from heaven" (1 Cor 15:47).

"From heaven," may refer to our Lord's coming in association with his incarnation, but in the context seems more likely to be a reference to a prospective appearance, at which time "the Lord Jesus Christ... will transform our lowly body to be like his glorious body" (Phil 3:20–21). Adam is put to sleep and his side opened so that the rib taken from him might be formed into a woman for him; Jesus is put to death and his side pierced so that the water and blood which flow from him might, after a long gestation, constitute the woman being prepared for him.

None of this, however, precludes a lightning-like appearance of the Son of man in the heavens. He himself is the destiny of his bride, the goal toward which she is tending. He is coming both "down from heaven" and "out from the womb of the Church" to meet her even as she is coming forth to meet him. His manifestation to her will undoubtedly be a sudden one. Writing to those who "wait for [God's] Son from heaven, whom he raised from the dead, Jesus who delivers us from the wrath to come" (1 Thess 1:10), St. Paul reminds them that "the day of the Lord will come like a thief in the night" (1 Thess 5:2). Having said this, he goes on to emphasize its abruptness as follows: "While people are saying, 'there is peace and security,' then sudden destruction will come upon them as labor pains come upon a pregnant woman" (1 Thess 5:3). The coming of the Lord is like the onset of birth pangs because, once more, he has come to birth and is ready to come forth.

The sudden nature of his arrival is comparable to the "precipitation" of a child from the womb and birth canal, or even the sudden falling of rain. As an example of the former, we might take the birth of children to Hebrew mothers in Egypt. When Pharaoh demanded an explanation from the midwives as to why Israelite boys were surviving childbirth in defiance of his command that they be put to death, the midwives replied that their mothers "give birth before the midwife comes to them" (Exod 1:19). Likewise, St. Paul seems to have had in mind that occasional case where the onset of a woman's pangs is followed swiftly and directly by the delivery of the child.[24]

To use the second analogy, when the air reaches its dew point, moisture precipitates in the form of dew or rain. The Scriptures actually compare the coming of the Lord to this precipitation of moisture from the atmosphere. "I will be like dew to Israel," the Lord promises through the prophet Hosea (Hos 14:6). The psalmist says of the king, "May he be like rain that falls on the mown grass, like showers that water the earth" (Ps 72:6). "Drop down dew, ye heavens," we read in the Roman breviary, "and let the clouds rain the Just One!" Perhaps when our collective capacity for embodying or manifesting Christ is reached, at that point he will suddenly return.

Prior to the first coming of Christ, Israel's hope found expression in two forms: apocalyptic, which anticipated God's direct intervention; and adherence to the law, which "envisioned a kingdom which man's righteousness could, if not produce, at least precipitate."[25] Those two forms of hope are still current, but require modification. God is already intervening directly (in and through the Church) to bring forth, not a state of affairs, but a person, whose righteousness he makes it the privilege of human beings to participate in and display, not as though it were their own, but in open acknowledgement that it comes from and belongs to him. The precipitation of his second coming is thus brought on by him—that is, by that same person, Christ—in somewhat the same way that a child's development inside the womb precipitates its emergence, beyond its mother's control. She has

---

24. A story my father used to tell illustrates this. During his medical residency, he and another obstetrics resident—we'll call him "Johnson"—were called to the home of a woman in labor with her first child. My father's job was to heat water and get things ready for the delivery, while Johnson attended the patient. From the kitchen he called to his partner to ask if the woman was ready yet, and Johnson replied, "No, she's only dilated two fingers." A moment later my father heard a loud noise and ran to see what had happened. The baby had precipitated and was on the floor, and Johnson and the walls were covered with blood. From then on, my father recalled, his partner was known as "two-fingers Johnson."

25. Bright, *Kingdom of God*, 170.

contributed vitally to its formation and readiness, but the child is God's work, in which she has graciously been allowed to have a part.

The coming of Christ in glory is therefore directly linked to his being brought forth by his people. On the one hand, their final transformation individually into his image must await their coming into his presence at the resurrection of the righteous. But, on the other hand, the corporate formation of the Church as his bride, the body of Christ, will already be complete as the *sine qua non* of his second advent. While each of his children is privileged to bring forth Christ in her life, no individual attains to perfect Christ-likeness this side of his own death and resurrection. Yet the living Christ-manifestation of every child of God contributes to the adorning of the bride who is being prepared for her heavenly Bridegroom. When she is ready—that is, able to dress herself in that "fine linen, bright and pure" which is made of "the righteous deeds of the saints"—the time for the resurrection to life (John 5:29), the marriage of the Lamb (Rev 19:7), and the emergence of a new heaven and a new earth (Rev 21:1) will have come.

Epilogue

> When a woman is giving birth, she has sorrow because her hour has come, but when she has delivered the baby, she no longer remembers the anguish, for joy that a human being [*anthropos*] has been born into the world. *John 16:21*

WHAT OUR STUDY HAS shown is that this woman giving birth, spoken of by Jesus to his disciples in the upper room on the eve of his Passion, is, by turns, 1) Israel under the old covenant, personified in the blessed Virgin; 2) Jesus himself, on the cross and in his resurrection; 3) the one, holy, catholic and apostolic Church, as represented by the apostles; 4) each and every individual Christian; and 5) even the entire cosmos, enucleated in mother earth. Additionally, we have seen that the human being who is brought forth through the birth pangs of their collective sufferings is none other than the "male child . . . who is to rule all the nations with a rod of iron" (Rev 12:5), and who is also the "one mediator between God and men, the man [*anthropos*] Christ Jesus" (1 Tim 2:5).

Salvation history itself is metaphorically encapsulated in the form of a pregnancy leading to a live birth, of which God's promise to Eve of an offspring brought forth in pain is the conception, and the death/resurrection of Jesus the anticipatory fulfillment.

Therefore, to the question posed so often and addressed in so many books about human suffering, where is God when it hurts?, we offer St. Paul's words as answer: God is in Christ, reconciling the world to himself and bringing forth a new creation (2 Cor 5:17, 19), born out of the ruins of the old.

To our Lord Jesus Christ, who lives and reigns with the Father and the Holy Spirit, be all glory and honor, dominion and power, thanksgiving and blessing, forever and ever. Amen.

Appendix 1

The Bones of Joseph: A Case Study in Bringing Forth Christ

WE HAVE SEEN[1] THAT St. Paul interprets his own sufferings in the course of his ministry as birth pangs. "My little children," he addresses the Galatians, "with whom I am again in the anguish of childbirth!" (Gal 4:19). The purpose of his pain—"until Christ is formed in you"—turns out to be nothing less than a gestation within his readers (mirroring that which is taking place within himself) that will lead ultimately to the revelation of Jesus through them. Just how this will happen he does not say, but a kind of parable of how Christ is formed and brought forth within his Church is provided us in St. John's narrative of the encounter between Jesus and a Samaritan woman, related in the fourth chapter of his Gospel.

In what comes immediately before, the disciples of John the baptizer question their master about Jesus and he answers, "You yourselves bear me witness, that I said, 'I am not the Christ, but I have been sent before him. The one who has the bride is the bridegroom'" (John 3:28–29). What the baptizer means by the bride is not entirely clear,[2] but the next thing we are told is that Jesus, on his way from Judea to Galilee, has stopped to talk to a Samaritan woman, leading us to wonder if what follows is not in some sense St. John's clarification of the answer to precisely that question.

---

1. In chapter 4.
2. Most likely it is the Church (Rev 19:7; 21:2).

The Land Given to Joseph

The location of their conversation is Jacob's well[3] (John 4:6), apparently just outside a town of Samaria called Sychar (John 4:5), given that the disciples leave Jesus at the well to go into the city to buy food (John 4:8). The town itself, St. John tells us, is "near the field that Jacob had given to his son Joseph." The significance of this seemingly extraneous information will become clear momentarily, but for now let us simply recall some relevant details, knowledge of which the writer of the Gospel has assumed on the part of his readers.

Upon returning to Canaan from Aram, where for years he worked for his brother-in-law, Jacob settled in the town of Shechem, on a piece of land which he bought for a hundred pieces of silver (Gen 33:18–19). Years later, after he had taken refuge in Egypt and become an old man, he said to his son Joseph, "Behold, I am about to die, but God will be with you and will bring you to the land of your fathers. Moreover, I have given to you rather than to your brothers one mountain slope [*shekem*[4]] that I took from the hand of the Amorites with my sword and with my bow" (Gen 48:21–22).

In his turn, Joseph, when he came to the end of his life, said to his brothers, "I am about to die, but God will visit you and bring you up out of this land to the land that he swore to Abraham, to Isaac, and to Jacob" (Gen 50:24). Then he proceeded to put the sons of Israel on oath, saying, "God will surely visit you, and you shall carry up my bones from here" (Gen 50:25). At the age of one hundred and ten he died, was embalmed, and was laid in a coffin in Egypt.

Four hundred years later, we read that as the Israelites departed from Egypt on the night of the first Passover, Moses, being reminded of the oath sworn by Jacob's sons to their brother, took with him "the bones of Joseph" (Exod 13:19).[5] These remains were carried by the Israelites throughout their forty years of wandering in the wilderness, and accompanied them into the promised land. Once the conquest of the land was accomplished under

---

3. Nowhere mentioned by that name in the patriarchal narratives, its exact location, according to Lindars (*Gospel of John*, 179), is not known.

4. Or "portion." Jacob is making a play on the Hebrew word for shoulder (*sekem*), apportioning the promised land like he might the roasted lamb at a family meal.

5. To which, according to Westermann (*Genesis 37–50*, 209), the *Testament of the Twelve Patriarchs* attributed an importance not unlike that given to the pillar of fire and the column of smoke (Exod 13:21–22). Gareth Lloyd-Jones makes of these bones a "metaphor for tradition" (Lloyd-Jones, *Bones of Joseph*, 3),

Joshua's leadership, Joseph's bones were finally laid to rest at Shechem,[6] in the very plot of ground purchased by Jacob and given to him, which became "an inheritance of the descendants of Joseph" (Josh 24:32).

This background justifies us in surmising that Jacob's well and the burial place of Joseph were quite likely in close proximity to each other. In any case, the ground upon which Jesus encountered the woman was, by St. John's allusion to Jacob's gift of it to Joseph, invested with extraordinary significance. Not only was Jesus "symbolically situated at the very place where Israel may be expected to enter upon her rightful inheritance,"[7] but the bones of Joseph were presumably resting still in the ground nearby.

It is safe to infer that Jesus, a careful student of the Scriptures and traditions of his people, was aware of at least as much about the background of the site as St. John assumes his readers to be. For her part, the Samaritan woman, being a resident of the area, might be presumed to be even better informed about the details, given that the Samaritans not only "laid great store by their connections with the scene of the patriarch's transaction,"[8] but also held Joseph in particularly high esteem. After all, the tribes associated with him by means of his sons—Ephraim and Manassah—originally occupied the land that later became Samaria,[9] and according to Josephus, the Samaritans claim to be their descendants.[10]

The Way of a Man with a Woman

According to St. John, Jesus arrived at the well at about noon (John 4:6). Because he was tired from his journey, he sat down there, and his disciples left him on an errand (John 4:8). When a woman approached to draw water, Jesus asked her to quench his thirst (John 4:7). With this request began a fascinating and highly enigmatic exchange.[11]

---

6. Shechem is important as the first place in Canaan where God appeared to Abraham and promised to give the land to his descendants (Gen 12:6–7). The "oldest part of the Holy Land to belong to the Israelites by right of purchase" (Lindars, *Gospel of John*, 179), it is probably regarded by Jacob as "a pledge of the future possession of the whole land" (Keil and Delitzsch, *Pentateuch*, 386).

7. Marsh, *Saint John*, 209.

8. Lindars, *Gospel of John*, 179.

9. MacDonald, *Theology of the Samaritans*, 15.

10. Schnackenburg, *Gospel According to St. John*, 1:429.

11. For an interesting commentary on the nuances of the conversation as a communication event, see Chappuis, "Jesus and the Samaritan Woman," 8–24.

Jesus avows that his purpose, in offering the woman "living water," is to communicate to her "who it is that is saying to you, 'Give me a drink'" (John 4:10). She has already identified him as a Jew, and she responds by implying his inferiority to "our father Jacob" (John 4:12).[12] It is only when Jesus directs her to "go, call your husband" (John 4:16) that intimations of his true identity begin to dawn on her. For the first time she understands the meaning of what he says. "I have no husband," she replies, to which Jesus responds, "You are right in saying, 'I have no husband'; for you have had five husbands, and the one you now have is not your husband" (John 4:17–18).

St. John's manner of presentation suggests that Jesus wants the woman not only to confront her implied promiscuity/adultery,[13] but to recognize that she has not yet found her true husband, the spouse for whom she is intended. This recognition is precisely what he achieves when the woman makes the frank, unguarded admission that she is unmarried. Up until this point, we might well imagine that she is like the promiscuous woman who "eats and wipes her mouth and says, 'I have done no wrong'" (Prov 30:20). Jesus, however, brings her to realization of her need.

Immediately preceding the verse from Proverbs just quoted, the writer lists four things that are "too wonderful for me," the last of which is "the way of a man with a virgin" (Prov 30:18–19). Although she is no virgin, this saying might serve as a gloss on the encounter between Jesus and the Samaritan woman. Like a man wooing his beloved, he seeks to win her to himself.[14] In fact, Jesus's interaction with the woman follows the conventions of a specific type-scene familiar from the patriarchal narratives of the Old Testament: the encounter of a suitor with an eligible woman at a well (Gen 29:1–14; Exod 2:6–22). Here, Jesus is the suitor, and this woman his intended.[15] If any symbolism is in the mind of the evangelist, J. N. Sanders writes, it is "that of the Savior seeking the Church, his bride."[16] The woman is not merely the representative Samaritan, but a representative of "the

---

12. The Greek construction of the question she puts to him (*me su meizon ei;*) anticipates a negative answer: "You're not greater, are you?"

13. Not all interpreters agree that this particular exchange constitutes censure of the woman's private life. Odeberg (*Fourth Gospel*, 186) endorses "the symbolical interpretation" that her "husbands" are the gods of the nations whose people settled Samaria after the forced exile of the majority of its Israelite inhabitants in the eighth century BCE.

14. Compare the relationship between the lover and his beloved in Song 5:2–8.

15. Marsh, *Saint John*, 207, 214; Brodie, *Gospel According to John*, 218; Brown, *Gospel According to John (I–XII)*, 171.

16. Sanders, *Commentary on St. John's Gospel*, 144.

whole body of believers"[17]—in the words of St. Augustine, "a model of the Church."[18] "The basic clue to this corporate role," one observer has said, "is the fact that in the narrative the role of the woman is intertwined with that of the disciples," whose mission is encased in hers.[19]

"Sir, I perceive that you are a prophet," the woman says to Jesus (John 4:19), acknowledging his prescience and moving closer to a recognition of his true identity. Out of deference to him who—she is perhaps beginning to realize—just may be "greater than our father Jacob" (and also possibly to divert the conversation from personal affairs), she places before him the controversy between her people and the Jews about the proper place for the worship of God. Then, rather than endorse Jesus's assertion that salvation is "from the Jews" (John 4:22), she withholds judgment, averring that when Messiah—"he who is called Christ"—comes, "he will tell us all things" (John 4:25).

The Samaritan Messiah

We must pause here to ask just what this woman means when she speaks of "Messiah." Because the Samaritans accept only the Pentateuch (the first five books of the Hebrew Scriptures) as canonical, their messianic tradition derives not at all from the Prophets and the Writings—and certainly not from David and the house of Judah (as does the contemporary Jewish tradition)—but primarily from Moses, the great prophet who is the deliverer of his people.[20] The distinctive Samaritan expectation is apparently of a *ta'eb*, or restorer, "a prophet like [Moses]" (Deut 18:15), that is, a Moses *redivivus* whose return will bring vindication to their cult and temple at Mount Gerazim, and destruction for its enemies.

It is apparent that St. John's Gospel, in particular, evinces a distinction in the mind of the Jews between the expected Messiah and "the prophet" awaited by them (John 1:19-28). According to one commentator, "in some places the prophet is distinguished from the Messiah (John 1:25; 7:40), and in another place apparently identified with him (John 6:14)." "It is of interest," he continues, "that Jewish expectations concerning Moses took

17. Marsh, *Saint John*, 212-23.
18. Augustine, *Homilies on the Gospel of John*, 284.
19. Brodie, *Gospel According to John*, 217.
20. Gaster, *Samaritans: Their History*, 89-91; Montgomery, *Samaritans: Earliest Jewish Sect*, 247.

two forms; and that while some looked for a second deliverer, a Messiah conceived along Mosaic lines, others thought of a return of Moses as a forerunner of the Messiah."[21] This, of course, says nothing about the nature of the Samaritans' expectations, but it possibly indicates that in Johannine theology—which may have been imputed by St. John to the Samaritans—"a prophet like Moses" is not identical to the Messiah.

Now, it is true that Joseph himself is never explicitly identified with the shadowy figure known as *Ta'eb*. Nevertheless, there is a tradition that the latter "was to come of the house of Joseph, the first 'king' of Israel, and inherit that leader's royal qualities,"[22] and the reign of the *Ta'eb* is compared to that of Joseph in Egypt.[23] Later Jewish tradition, it seems, does admit the coming of a "Messiah-ben-Joseph" ("son of Joseph," that is, of his tribe) whose "particular duty [is] to collect and lead home the scattered Ten Tribes" before the advent of "Messiah–ben–David."[24] In the view of Sigmund Mowinckel, the notion of a "Messiah-ben-Joseph"

> might well be thought [to have arisen] among the Samaritans as a counterpart of the Jewish Messiah of the house of David, but ... it was occasionally accepted in Jewish circles, partly because it could claim support from the interpretation of certain passages of Scripture, [and] partly because the Jews could regard the Messiah-ben-Joseph as one of the forerunners of the Messiah, like "Taxo" of the house of Levi, whose task it was to lead home the dispersed members of the ten tribes.[25]

It is possible, on the other hand, Mowinckel says, that "the concept arose from what is said in Obadiah about the house of Joseph, which will become a flame and consume Edom" (Obad 18). Alternatively, it may have a more concrete origin in the dynasty of Galilean messiahs (especially Menachem-ben-Hezekiah), who "gave rise to the thought of a dying Messiah-ben-Joseph, all of whom fell in conflict with Rome, which was at that time regarded as the fulfillment of the prophecy about Gog and Magog, or as Edom." This latter is an attractive explanation, because "it is explicitly stated that the Messiah-ben-Joseph will appear in upper Galilee."[26]

21. Glasson, *Moses in the Fourth Gospel*, 27.
22. Montgomery, *Samaritans: Earliest Jewish Sect*, 248.
23. Montgomery, *Samaritans: Earliest Jewish Sect*, 368.
24. Gaster, *Samaritans: Their History*, 91–92.
25. Mowinckel, *He That Cometh*, 290.
26. Mowinckel, *He That Cometh*, 291.

APPENDIX 1: THE BONES OF JOSEPH

One study of the Moses traditions in St. John's Gospel finds that references to Joseph's kingship are frequent in fourth-century-CE sources, and concludes that, at least in that era, "the kingdom of Joseph is the kingdom to which the Samaritans belong."[27] Moreover, there are, according to Meeks, several passages, based on Exodus 19:6,[28] "which speak of all the Samaritans as kings, whose kingdom began with the Exodus." At this later date, he says, Moses was regarded as the restorer of the "kingdom of Joseph," which belonged to all Israel (that is, the Samaritans) but was lost in Egypt.[29]

The Samaritan messiah is, therefore, an ambiguous figure. "Nothing definite is said about him," one writer admits; "even his character and activity are only indicated in general outlines, and he is just as dim and vague as the whole eschatology of the Samaritans."[30] As one who is expected to "tell us all things," according to the Samaritan woman's expectation, he might, in one commentator's view, be thought to have at least as much in common with Joseph as with Moses.[31] It is Joseph, after all, who, having been sold into Egypt by his brothers and put in prison there on a false charge, rises to a position of responsibility and correctly interprets the enigmatic dreams of two of Pharaoh's imprisoned officials (Gen 40:1–13). And when Pharaoh himself has disturbing dreams (Gen 41:1–8), he summons Joseph to give him the interpretation. "God has revealed to Pharaoh what he is going to do," Joseph tells him (Gen 41:25), to which Pharaoh replies approvingly, "Can we find a man like this, in whom is the Spirit of God?" (Gen 41:38). Joseph is thus made governor of all Egypt, and when a severe famine occurs over the whole region, his father and the same brothers who tried to kill him find refuge with him, and their lives are preserved.

We are reminded of the miracle of the loaves, especially as it is recounted in the John's Gospel. According to St. John, the crowd that receives the benefits of that miracle, remembering no doubt Moses and the manna, takes Jesus to be "the prophet who is to come into the world" (John 6:14).

---

27. Meeks, *Prophet-King*, 228.
28. "You shall be to me a kingdom of priests and a holy nation."
29. Meeks, *Prophet-King*, 230–31.
30. Gaster, *Samaritans: Their History*, 90–91.
31. Montgomery, *Samaritans: Earliest Jewish Sect*, 243. It is clear, according to Meeks (*Prophet-King*, 223), that "for the Samaritans, Moses's prophetic office consisted in the revelation of heavenly secrets through him." But he also mentions (250) that "events reported by Josephus (*Antiquities*, 18:85) indicate a popular Samaritan hope that someone associated with Moses in a way no longer clear would recover the hidden cult implements of the Gerazim temple making possible the restoration of true worship."

But John goes on to say that Jesus realizes that they were about to come and take him by force and "make him king" (John 6:15). The association here of prophet and king seems to point as much to Joseph as to Moses as a messianic figure.[32] In fact, upon close examination of the Johannine tradition, we find that the figure of the patriarch Joseph lies quite prominently in the background of the Gospel as a whole.

It is St. John's distinctive emphasis on the opposition of Jesus's family (particularly his brothers, John 7:3–5), taken together with the characteristic conflict between Jesus and the Jews (5:18; 7:1; 8:39–59; 10:31–39; 11:45–53), that is most strongly redolent of Joseph and his story. As a young man, Joseph brings his father a bad report about his brothers (Gen 37:2). This, coupled with their jealousy (Gen 37:11) because of Jacob's preference for him (Gen 37:33), causes them to hate him (Gen 37:4). Their hatred is exacerbated by Joseph's dreams, in which he claims prerogatives offensive to them (Gen 37:5–11), eventually leading to their plot against him (Gen 37:18–20). By the same token, Jesus's conflict with the Jews—who are the descendants of Joseph's brothers, and in particular, of Judah, their leader—intensifies until the Jews obtain his condemnation and death sentence (John 18:12–16). Just as Joseph later supplies his brothers with food and a place to live in Goshen, the most fertile part of Egypt (Gen 45:16–20; 46:28), so Jesus provides food both before (John 6:1–11) and after (John 21:1–13) his death, and promises to prepare a place "in my Father's house" where he will "take you to myself" (John 14:2).

The overall resemblance of Jesus to Joseph throughout St. John's Gospel is unmistakable, adding to the likelihood that there is some such influence at work on the narrative of Jesus's encounter with the Samaritan woman. While it is true that Moses, the prototype of the Samaritan messiah, is also prominent in the Johannine picture, the emphasis in his case seems to be more on his contrast with than his similarity to Jesus, as when, for example, St. John writes, "the law was given through Moses," but "grace and truth came through Jesus Christ" (John 1:17).[33] And when Jesus says that Moses "wrote of me" (John 5:46), we can as easily understand that to be a reference to the Joseph narrative in Genesis—commonly attributed in Jesus's time to the authorship of Moses—as an allusion to "a prophet like me."

---

32. We note that, before his own death, Moses himself pronounces a blessing "on the head of Joseph, who is prince among his brothers" (Deut 33:16), suggesting both a kingly crown and a royal anointing.

33. Compare the remark of Jesus to the effect that "it was not Moses who gave you the bread from heaven" (John 6:32).

APPENDIX 1: THE BONES OF JOSEPH

As we have seen, the writings of Moses characterize Joseph as the revealer of the meaning of God's mysteries. "The LORD was with Joseph," not only to "cause all that he did to succeed" (Gen 39:2–3, 21, 23), but also to enable him to understand the secret meanings of things that come from God. When Pharaoh's officials come to him perplexed over the significance of their dreams, Joseph asks them, "Do not interpretations belong to God?" (Gen 40:8). When none of Pharaoh's magicians or wise men can interpret his dreams, the chief cupbearer, whom Joseph rightly prophesied would be released from prison and returned to royal favor (Gen 40:9–15, 20–21), remembers the young Hebrew in prison who told him exactly what his dream meant. Pharaoh calls Joseph and says, "I have heard it said of you that when you hear a dream you can interpret it" (Gen 41:15). This ability to explain mysteries and foretell events seems to agree with the Samaritan woman's concept of a prophetic Messiah.

The question becomes one of whether the woman sees Jesus as a "Moses" or a "Joseph." If later sources may be relied upon to point us toward a solution, we may conclude that we do not need to choose between the two. One observer, drawing upon the fourth-century-CE writings of a Samaritan named Marqah, finds evidence that Joseph and Moses are closely associated in the thinking of the Samaritans,[34] which, because of the extremely conservative nature of the cult, is unlikely to have changed significantly over the three to four centuries that had elapsed since the time of Jesus. "It is apparent," he writes, "that in Marqah's view it was Moses who restored the kingdom of Joseph through the Exodus." Furthermore, Joseph, Moses, and the *Ta'eb* are connected in the following passage from Midrash Marqah:

> The *Ta'eb* will come in peace to repossess the place which God chose for these good people. Joseph came; so he was recompensed with a kingdom after servitude and those who had oppressed him sought his favor . . . Where is there the like of Joseph, illumined, wise, possessing the spirit of God? He reigned over the place. Therefore his bones were borne by a prophet who was the faithful one of his Lord's house. There is none like Joseph the king and there is none like Moses the prophet. Each of them possessed high status; Moses reigned over prophet-hood, Joseph reigned over the Goodly Mount[35]. There is none greater than either of them.[36]

---

34. Meeks, *Prophet-King*, 216–56.
35. Mount Gerazim, site of the Samaritan temple.
36. Meeks, *Prophet-King*, 230–31.

Along these lines, it may well be that the notion of Messiah held by the Samaritan woman who encounters Jesus is to be found in the following image, presented in the account of the exodus: "Moses took the bones of Joseph with him, for Joseph had made the sons of Israel solemnly swear, saying, 'God will surely visit you, and you shall carry up my bones with you from here'" (Exod 13:19). This action of Moses is explained as a response to the pledge that Joseph exacts from his brothers, the sons of Israel, just before he dies (Gen 50:24–25). In taking the responsibility upon himself, Moses acts on behalf of the people; and therefore, while it is the Lord who carries the people out of Egypt on eagles' wings (Exod 19:4), it is Moses who transports Joseph. We submit that Jesus is, for the Samaritan woman, this *Ta'eb*, this "Moses": the Moses who bears Joseph's bones, and we venture the distinction that Moses is a type, or figure, of Christ living, whereas Joseph's bones represent Christ dead.

Jesus and Joseph

It was left to the Israelites, after the death of Moses and after their entry into the promised land, to bury these bones of Joseph in the ground "at Shechem, in the piece of ground that Jacob bought" (Josh 24:32), somewhere nearby the well to which the Samaritan woman comes to draw water. Jesus now, in a mystical way, exhumes them from the place where they have lain all these years that he might implant them within the woman, and in so doing, reproduce Joseph in her. Moses was not capable of doing this,[37] but Jesus—as "Moses" bearing that "Joseph" who gave life to his family when they were nearly dead from hunger—is able, especially since Joseph is a figure, or type, of Jesus himself. "Who is he before whom parents and brothers bowed down to the ground," St. Ambrose asks, referring to the incident recorded in Genesis 37:5–11, "but Jesus Christ?"[38]

This latter assertion requires some explanation. With the single exception of the passage under consideration, the patriarch Joseph is not mentioned by name in the Gospels, nor is Jesus compared to him elsewhere in the New Testament.[39] Nevertheless, as is widely acknowledged,

---

37. "If a law had been given that could give life, then then righteousness would indeed be by the law" (Gal 3:21).

38. Ambrose, "Joseph," 271. Therefore, Joseph both goes down into Egypt in order to save his family and comes out of Egypt with them (Hos 11:1).

39. As he is to Moses (Heb 3:1–5).

the career and character of Joseph do present unmistakable parallels to the life and ministry of Jesus. "We may," say two Old Testament scholars, "without hesitation look upon the history of Joseph as a type of the pathway . . . of Christ, from lowliness to exaltation, from slavery to liberty, from suffering to glory . . . We may also, so far as the history of Israel is a type of the history of Christ and his church, regard the life of Joseph, as believing commentators of all centuries have done, as a type of the life of Christ."[40] "Christian exegetes have often seen Joseph as a type of Christ," Gordon Wenham has said: "the innocent man who through his suffering brings reconciliation to his human brethren and life to the world."[41]

The synopsis of the history of Joseph given in Psalm 105 seems prophetic, or at least prescient, of Jesus. When God "summoned a famine on the land and broke all supply of bread" (Ps 105:6) we are told, "he had sent a man ahead of them, Joseph, who was sold as a slave. His feet were hurt with fetters, his neck was put in a collar of iron; until what he had said came to pass, the word of the LORD tested him. The king sent and released him; the ruler of the peoples set him free; he made him lord of his house and ruler of all his possessions, to bind his princes at his pleasure, and to teach his elders wisdom" (Ps 105:17–22). In retrospect, it does not require much imagination to find here intimations of the career of Jesus as it is summarized by St. Paul in the second chapter of his letter to the Philippians.

> Have this mind among yourselves, which is yours in Christ Jesus, who, though he was in the form of God, did not count equality with God a thing to be grasped, but made himself nothing, taking the form of a servant, being born in the likeness of men. And being found in human form, he humbled himself by becoming obedient to the point of death, even death on a cross. Therefore God has highly exalted him and bestowed on him the name that is above every name, so that at the name of Jesus every knee should bow, in heaven and on earth and under the earth, and every tongue confess that Jesus Christ is Lord, to the glory of God the Father. (Phil 2:5–11)

Jesus himself seems to draw on the similarities between them in his teaching, particularly when he speaks of the treatment that he receives at the hands of the Jewish leaders. To take but one example from the synoptic tradition, it is not difficult to detect in the parable of the wicked tenants as

---

40. Keil and Delitzsch, *Pentateuch*, 334.
41. Wenham, *Genesis 16–50*, 360.

APPENDIX 1: THE BONES OF JOSEPH

related by St. Mark (Mark 12:1–11) some echoes of the story of Joseph's treatment at the hands of his brothers. The owner of the vineyard bears a resemblance to Jacob (with the minor difference that Jacob's property was in sheep rather than grapes). There is nothing to compare with the servants sent by the absentee owner, but certainly the "beloved son" (Mark 12:6) whom he finally sends reminds us of Joseph—the first-born of Rachel, and therefore specially loved by Jacob (Gen 37:3)—sent by his father to pay his brothers a visit (Gen 37:12–14). Jesus's brothers conspire against him, as do the tenants in the parable, and though the former do not kill Joseph—only making it look like he has been killed (Gen 37:31–33)—they do, in effect, throw him out of the vineyard (Mark 12:8) by having him taken off into Egypt (Gen 37:28). Since Jesus directs this parable against those Jews who are opposing and trying to kill him (Mark 11:18), and since the latter are represented by the tenants, those tenants can easily be equated with Jacob's other ten sons. According to this interpretation, then, Joseph is clearly a type of Jesus, especially if his being cast into a pit is emblematic of death (a symbolism certainly native to the context of the story), and if his being taken out of it alive (Gen 37:28) speaks of a kind of resurrection.

Meanwhile, the Samaritan woman is waiting for the Ta'eb to explain everything to her. Jesus will be her true spouse when he comes. He has now moved her to the place where she can receive—and bear—the revelation of who he is.[42] "I who speak to you," he says, "am he"—that is, that "Messiah" who is coming and "will tell [you] all things" (John 4:25–26). It is as though, in effect, he is saying, "I am your true husband. I have already begun to tell you everything, and in so doing I have known you as only a husband can know his wife."[43] For her part, the woman has, without fully realizing

---

42. The suspense that has built to this point, and the dramatic tension that is released by his announcement, is highly reminiscent of the same suspense and tension that precede Joseph's revelation of his true identity to his unsuspecting and astounded brothers (Gen 45:1–3).

43. How this is possible, given the fact that, to use St. John's own words, "Jews . . . have no dealings with Samaritans" (John 4:9), may actually be hinted at elsewhere in his Gospel. When Jesus is accused by his opponents of being a Samaritan and having a demon (John 8:48), his reply ignores the first charge and addresses only the second: "I do not have a demon," he says (John 8:49). If his silence regarding the first may be interpreted as a form of consent (to its spirit, if not to its letter), then Jesus in effect associates himself with the despised sect. As in some sense, then, a Samaritan himself (Luke 10:33), he is all the more fitted to be this woman's husband (John 4:16–18) and to form himself within her.

it, received him as such, in what Brodie has called a "betrothal of belief."[44] This reception is not explicitly stated, but presumably it takes place in the form of her inward response to Jesus's command, "Woman, believe me"[45] (John 4:21)—that is, as a kind of Samaritan "let it be to me according to your word" (Luke 1:38). It is, at any rate, a moment of conception.

To understand this, it is helpful to recall a bit more of the story of Joseph's father Jacob as we find it in the Genesis narrative. That he is a familiar figure to the Samaritan woman is clear from her reference to him in her conversation with Jesus. "Are you greater," she has asked, "than our father Jacob?" (John 4:12). Not only had Jacob given the Samaritans the well at which Jesus finds her, but he himself once came to a well (Gen 29:1–2), like Jesus, at "high day" (Gen 29:7). He too met a woman there, who approached after he arrived (Gen 29:6, 9). Instead of asking her for water as Jesus does, however, Jacob proceeded to water her flock for her (Gen 29:10), in anticipation, we may perhaps say, of Jesus's promise to give water to the woman.

Jacob, moreover, fell in love with the shepherdess (Gen 29:18), whose name was Rachel, and was betrothed to her (Gen 29:19–20), prefiguring the spiritual espousal between Jesus and the Samaritan woman—who, as it happens, will shepherd her fellow townspeople to him (John 4:28–29). Rachel, it turns out, was barren (Gen 29:31), but eventually conceived and bore a son for Jacob to whom she gave the name "Joseph" (*Yoseph*,[46] Gen. 30:24), even as the Samaritan woman now conceives, as it were, a "second Joseph"—that "additional" son (Benjamin, "son of the right hand," Gen 35:18) whom Rachel had prayed for—as a result of her encounter with Jesus.

Jesus is, we might say, reproducing himself in the Samaritan woman. We are speaking, of course, in spiritual terms. The agency of the action is therefore the Holy Spirit, that living water which Jesus would have given to her in response to her request (John 4:10), and which she has now received. But he does not undertake to do this in abstraction from the circumstances in which they meet, foremost among which is the ground—literally—upon which they stand. The bones of Joseph which rest somewhere nearby correspond to the concept of Messiah (*Ta'eb*) which comes from her Scriptures

44. Brodie, *Gospel According to John*, 218.

45. Interestingly, this appears to be the only instance where the imperative *pisteue moi* (believe [in] me), is addressed by Jesus to a particular individual, who is at the same time addressed as *gynai*, woman.

46. From the Hebrew root *yasaph* meaning "add" or "increase," in token of her request that "the Lord add to me another son."

APPENDIX 1: THE BONES OF JOSEPH

and which the woman has pondered in her heart. The incipient formation of Christ which immediately follows his conception within her is therefore a kind of coming together of just these bones. This itself is a mysterious thing. "As you do not know the way the Spirit comes to the bones in the womb of a woman with child," says the author of Ecclesiastes, "so you do not know the work of God who makes everything" (Eccl 11:5).[47]

It calls to mind the great vision of the prophet Ezekiel, who is set down by "the Spirit of the LORD" in the middle of a valley full of bones (Ezek 37:1), representing the exiled nation of Israel. Ezekiel is commanded, "Prophesy over these bones, and say to them, O dry bones, hear the word of the LORD. Thus says the Lord God to these bones: Behold, I will cause breath to enter you, and you shall live. And I will lay sinews upon you, and will cause flesh to come upon you, and cover you with skin, and put breath in you, and you shall live, and you shall know that I am the LORD" (Ezek 37:4–6).

Ezekiel does as he is ordered, and while he is prophesying, "there was a sound, and behold, a rattling, and the bones came together, bone to its bone" (Ezek 37:7). As he looks, "Behold, there were sinews on them, and flesh had come upon them, and skin had covered them" (Ezek 37:8). The imagery is strikingly similar to that of an embryo or fetus being formed within the womb. And yet the picture is also one of resurrection:

> Then he said to me, Son of man, these bones are the whole house of Israel. Behold, they say, Our bones are dried up, and our hope is lost; we are indeed cut off. Therefore prophesy and say to them, Thus says the LORD God: Behold, I will open your graves and raise you from your graves, O my people. And I will bring you into the land of Israel. And you shall know that I am the LORD, when I open your graves and raise you from your graves, O my people. And I will put my Spirit within you, and you shall live, and I will place you in your own land. Then you shall know that I am the LORD; I have spoken, and I will do it, declares the LORD. (Ezek 37:11–14)

The scene takes place, presumably, in or near Babylon, during the exile. But the dry bones may well contain an allusion to the bones of Joseph, carried out in a kind of resurrection at the time of the exodus, "brought

---

47. The mother of the seven sons put to death by Antiochus Epiphanes expresses a similar sentiment when she addresses them during their martyrdom: "I do not know how you appeared in my womb; it was not I who endowed you with breath and life, I had not the shaping of your every part" (2 Macc 7:22, New Jerusalem Bible translation).

back into the land of Israel" and "placed in your own land."[48] If this can be related, then, to the case of the Samaritan woman, we can certainly see some remarkable parallels. She comes to the well in the first place because, metaphorically speaking, her "bones are dried up," that is, like the Israel of which Ezekiel speaks, her hope is lost, and as a Samaritan she is indeed cut off by being alienated from the Jews through whom alone, according to what Jesus says to her, salvation is to come (John 4:22). By speaking to her, Jesus raises her from her grave, puts his Spirit within her, and places her in her own land.[49] And just as surely as the Israelites "shall know" that he who both speaks and does this is none other than "the LORD," so does the Samaritan woman come to know that "I who speak to you"—and do these things for you—"am he" (John 4:26).

A Fruitful Plant Near a Spring

Jesus no sooner says this to her than his disciples arrive at the well (John 4:27). Finding him in conversation with a woman, they are surprised. Whereas we might have expected them to challenge her right of access to their master, for some reason they dare not do so. We can only speculate that they are dumbfounded by what they see before them: a woman transformed by her encounter with this man. If she speaks again to Jesus, her words are not recorded. St. John simply tells us that she leaves her water jar and hurries back to the town (John 4:28). What St. Paul says about himself—God "was pleased to reveal his Son to[50] me, in order that I might preach him among the Gentiles" (Gal 1:16)—applies retrospectively to what we are told of her. Like Paul, moreover, she does not "immediately consult with anyone."

---

48. Moreover, it is perhaps not altogether unlikely that, at the time of their Babylonian captivity, the Israelites once more took those well-travelled bones with them to a temporary resting place, again in foreign soil, so that Joseph might participate in another return at the restoration.

49. In the context of the imagery of childbearing in Isaiah 66, the prophet promises that, at the restoration of the nation, "your bones shall flourish like the grass" (Isa 66:14), implying an allusion to burial as a kind of planting (compare 2 Sam 7:10, where God promises to plant his people in the land) or at least dormancy, from which God will bring forth new life. This calls to mind not only the dry bones spoken of by Ezekiel, but also the bones of Joseph in their resting place in Shechem.

50. Greek *en*, lit., "in."

APPENDIX 1: THE BONES OF JOSEPH

The focus of the narrative now shifts to Jesus and his disciples. They are concerned that he has not eaten (John 4:31), but he says, "My food is to do the will of him who sent me, and to accomplish his work" (John 4:34). These words are a commentary on the fact that the woman has abandoned her water jar at the well and gone to the town to tell the people about the man who has known her. "Come," she says, "see a man who told me all that I ever did" (John 4:29). Her drink is now the same as his food: doing the will of the Father and completing his work. At the same time, Jesus's words are a rebuke of the disciples, who have been to the town, not to proclaim him to the inhabitants or invite them to come out to meet him, but to buy food (John 4:8) for themselves.

It is her going forth in his name, above all, that testifies to his being conceived and formed within her, in what one writer calls the "empty cradle" of her heart that has been "waiting for the birth of Christ to fill it": "Those who have him, those in whom he is born again day after day, have just this one work to do, to show the others that what they want, what they long for, is Christ."[51] The Samaritan woman shares Jesus's desire to complete his work. "Can this be the Christ?" she asks them (John 4:29), the form of the question (*meti houtos estin ho christos;*) inviting an affirmative answer. In order that she might bring them forth to him, she brings him forth to them. This man must indeed be Messiah because he is like that Joseph for whom they too are waiting. His bones have been raised up from the ground and he is speaking to them through this woman. So they can do nothing but make their way toward this Christ.

Meanwhile, Jesus watches and awaits their arrival. As he does so, he speaks again to his disciples: "Do you not say, 'There are yet four months, and then comes the harvest'? Look, I tell you, lift up your eyes, and see that the fields are white for harvest. Already the one who reaps is receiving wages and gathering fruit for eternal life, so that sower and reaper may rejoice together. For here the saying holds true, 'One sows and another reaps.' I sent you to reap that for which you did not labor. Others have labored, and you have entered into their labor" (John 4:35–38). If the Samaritans coming toward him are a field ready for harvest, then the woman is presumably the sower, and he, the reaper. The disciples are sent to reap something that they have had no part in bringing to harvest. By saying "others have labored [*kekopiakasin*]," Jesus possibly has in mind John the baptizer and all the prophets before him, but also the woman—and above

---

51. Houselander, *Mother of Christ*, 36.

APPENDIX 1: THE BONES OF JOSEPH

all, himself, given that St. John uses a form of the same word to describe Jesus's weary state (*kekopiakos*) when he arrives at the well. Whereas Ezekiel saw "an exceedingly great army" (Ezek 37:10) come to life and rise to its feet, Jesus sees a whole harvest in the many Samaritans who come out to him in response to the woman's testimony.

The imagery of sowing and reaping that Jesus employs here recalls the passage from Ecclesiastes quoted earlier, having to do with the mysterious knitting together of bones within a pregnant woman's womb. Bracketing that passage are the following sayings: "He who observes the wind will not sow, and he who regards the clouds will not reap" (Eccl 11:4), and "in the morning sow your seed, and at evening withhold not your hand" (Eccl 11:6). While the germination of seed is the main metaphor for the hiddenness or mystery of the kingdom in the gospel parables of Jesus (Mark 4:26–29, 30–32), in this passage from the Old Testament we find it coupled with the image of the formation of the embryo in the womb, which is in turn likened to the mysterious movement of the wind. For the writer of Ecclesiastes, indeed, wind (or spirit) is the principal mystery, exemplified primarily in fetal growth or development and only derivatively by seminal growth in the ground. In St. John's Gospel, Jesus employs the imagery of wind (John 3:8) and of a seed (John 12.24), but not—at least not in an overt or explicit way—that of the embryo. The seed sown is that "word of Christ" (Rom 10:17), which, implanted within, immediately begins to bring forth its fruit by both producing itself, as happens within the Samaritan woman, and reproducing itself, as happens—through her—within her fellow townspeople.

Her remarkable fruitfulness constitutes another link with the Messiah figure whom both the woman and the Samaritans of Sychar know as Joseph. In his final blessing of his sons before he died, Jacob characterizes Joseph as "a fruitful bough by a spring [*ayin*][52]," whose "branches run over the wall" (Gen 49:22). The motif of fruitfulness is also associated with the blessing on Joseph (or, more precisely, on the tribes of Ephraim and Manassah derived from him) that Moses pronounces at the end of his life: "Blessed by the LORD be his land, with the choicest gifts of heaven above, and of the deep that crouches beneath, with the choicest fruits of the sun and the rich yield of the months, with the finest produce of the ancient mountains and the abundance

---

52. The Septuagint follows a different text here, but this Hebrew term is commonly rendered elsewhere in Greek by *pege*, which is St. John's word for the well that serves as a meeting place for Jesus and the Samaritan woman (John 4:6).

of the everlasting hills, with the best gifts of the earth and its fullness, and the favor of him who dwells in the bush" (Deut 33:13–16).

As is well known, such blessings serve not so much a present as a future function, that is, they are a kind of prediction of what will be true—in this case, of those who trace their ancestry back to Joseph. Now, insofar as the people of Israel (and Samaria) reckon that ancestry according to their membership in one of the twelve tribes, they cannot properly claim Joseph, since no tribe is named after him. And yet, perhaps one reason for this seeming anomaly is the intention to make Joseph the conduit, so to speak, for the blessings that will come upon all the tribes.

In introducing the so-called "Joseph cycle" in the latter part of the Book of Genesis, the author makes use of the term *toledoth* (generations), which he previously applied at critical junctures to the creation narrative (Gen 2:4) and the table of descendants of Adam (Gen 5:1), Noah (Gen 6:9), Shem (Gen 10:1, 32), and Terah (Gen 11:10, 27). "These are the generations of Jacob," the narrator says (Gen 37:2). But instead of going on to give the genealogical record, as he has in the preceding chapter with the descendants of Esau (Gen 36:1) and in the other instances where the term occurs (with the exception of Gen 2:4, which is a unique case), he simply states the name "Joseph" and launches into his story, which—on the surface, at least—has no bearing on genealogy. The effect is to make Joseph the descendant of Jacob due to the fact that it is because of and through him that the family survives and therefore that the blessing of Jacob is passed on.

The blessing of Jacob, and indeed, all blessing, has its source in the original blessing given by God to his people, what St. Paul calls "the blessing of Abraham" (Gal 3:14; Gen 12:2), which is couched in terms of families (or clans): "I will bless those who bless you, and him who dishonors you I will curse, and in you all the families of the earth shall be blessed" (Gen 12:3). It is fitting, therefore, that the first family to receive a blessing, according to the Genesis narrative, is that of Jacob (also called Israel), to whom the blessing comes through Joseph, who rescues his family from famine and establishes it in a fertile region of Egypt. Moreover, through him that blessing of Abraham comes, as St. Paul says, to the Gentiles as well (Gal 3:14), that is—in an anticipatory fashion—to the Egyptians of that generation whom Joseph saves from starvation (Gen 41:53–57). In its ultimate outworking in Christ, as St. John's Gospel shows us, this extension of blessing continues through the Samaritan woman.

APPENDIX 1: THE BONES OF JOSEPH

In the woman, therefore, who can be said to claim Joseph in a special way because his bones are being knit together within her, the prophecy of Jacob finds its true fulfillment. The conceptual connection that we need to apprehend this more clearly is supplied by imagery in the psalms. There, the psalmist makes "Joseph" a designation for the entire people of Israel (Ps 80:1),[53] who are at the same time likened to a vine (Ps 80:8). Joseph is thus, for the psalmist as for the author of the concluding chapters of Genesis, associated with the image of the vine.[54] The planting of this vine in the land of Canaan may therefore be a metaphorical way of describing the burial of the bones of Joseph in the plot of ground at Shechem.

This is where the curious use of the word "bones" for the body of Joseph becomes instructive. As noted previously, it denotes not a mere skeleton but a fully preserved and embalmed corpse (Gen 50:26), just like that of his father Jacob (Gen 50:2). In fact, however, "bones" is not used of Jacob's corpse, in spite of the fact that their deaths are recorded one immediately after the other in the concluding chapters of Genesis, most likely by the same hand. A possible explanation is that by "bones" the author means to intimate, in Joseph's case, a dead body that, once borne out of Egypt, will in some sense live again. As one commentator has said, "we might even guess that Joseph's care for the disposal of his bones indicated according to our author a belief in the resurrection that was to come."[55]

Because she has been entrusted with the bones of Joseph, it falls to the Samaritan woman to be "a fruitful bough by a spring," from which she draws the living water that animates her and enables her branches to run over the

---

53. Not only is "Joseph" occasionally the name given to the Israelites in Hebrew psalmody (Pss 78:67; 81:5), but there is evidence that the Samaritans too thought of themselves as "Joseph." "The fact that Joseph's kingship is linked with his liberation" from prison in Egypt, observes Meeks (*Prophet-King*, 229), "suggests that in these traditions 'Joseph' is an eponym or type for the Israelite nation, that is, the Samaritans, who could speak of themselves, in distinction from the Jews, as the descendants of Joseph or Ephraim."

54. As, of course, is Jesus (John 15:1). Compare Rom 11:16-24, where Christ is likened to an olive tree, of which both Jews and Gentiles are branches.

55. Hanson, *Jesus Christ in the Old Testament*, 177. In biblical parlance, the word "bones" by itself may carry this hopeful connotation. In Matt 23:27, Jesus likens the Pharisees to "whitewashed tombs... full of dead people's bones." "Dead people's bones" appears to be a pleonasm (all bones in tombs are the bones of dead people), and yet Jesus may actually be distinguishing between bones of the dead (such as the Pharisees) and those of the living, between which a separation will be made at the time of the general resurrection (John 5:28-29). In the same sense, God is "not the God of the dead, but of the living" (Mark 12:27).

wall. On her, then, are bestowed the blessings foretold by Jacob for Joseph: "blessings of heaven above, blessings of the deep that crouches beneath, blessings of the breasts and of the womb" (Gen 49:25). Jesus reaches over the wall separating Samaritans from Jews, and women from men. The Samaritan woman not only imitates him but extends his work in both spheres. Because of her testimony, many Samaritans of Sychar believe in Jesus (John 4:39), and after they prevail upon him to remain with them for a few days, many more come to faith as well, "because of his word" (John 4:41). Having heard him for themselves, they know him to be not only the Christ, but "indeed the Savior of the world" (John 4:42). Already the woman's work of bringing forth this Messiah promises to reach out beyond them.

Appendix 2

Bringing Forth Jesus as *Imitatio Mariae*

"Giving birth to the Christ-child" as a metaphor for the process of sanctification has a long and venerable history in Christian tradition. This ought not to be at all surprising when we consider how deeply rooted the imagery of childbirth is in the Old Testament and in the developing notion of the travail known as the messianic woes. But it is the actual incarnation of God's Word in the womb of an individual that establishes the concrete basis upon which the metaphor becomes capable of rich elaboration.

The Virgin Mary, the Church, and the Soul

Because of her unique role as mother of our Lord, Mary became for the early fathers of the Church the model for an incipient theology of "bringing forth Jesus." According to Irenaeus, the blessed Virgin is "the womb of God," and since she stands for the church, the same imagery gradually came to be associated with it. Clement of Alexandria, in the late second or early third century, appears to have been the first to describe the Church as "Mother."[56] For his part, Origen may have been the first to suggest that the idea of motherhood applies to the individual believer as well as to the Church. For him, the latter was joined to her heavenly Spouse "so

---

56. Clement, *Instructor*, 42.

APPENDIX 2: BRINGING FORTH JESUS AS IMITATIO MARIAE

that she may conceive by him and be saved through this chaste begetting of children . . . brought forth by the spotless Church or by the soul that seeks nothing bodily . . . but is aflame with the single love of the Word of God."[57] St. Augustine made this more explicit: "Do in the chambers of your soul, what you view with amazement in the flesh of Mary. He who believes in his heart unto justice conceives Christ; he who with his mouth makes profession of faith unto salvation brings forth Christ."[58] "The Word of God," said Maximus the Confessor, "desires to realize in everyone the mystery of his incarnation."[59]

Perhaps it was inevitable that individual Christians began to be thought of as wombs for bringing Jesus into the world. "In her spiritual conceiving and motherhood by faith, which preceded and co-existed with her physical conceiving and motherhood of Jesus," writes Eric Doyle, "Mary is the model for every disciple of her Son, [who also] becomes a mother of Christ."[60] This notion flowered in the Middle Ages, as exemplified in the twelfth-century writings of one Guerric, Cistercian abbot of Igny. Guerric was aware of the "old and long tradition," ultimately based on such passages as Mark 3:33–34[61] and Luke 11:28,[62] that "we are to share with Mary her motherhood of Christ."[63] "If Mary is the type of the Church," he wrote, "she is the type of the [Christian] soul." In the Cistercian tradition stemming from St. Bernard, bishops and abbots were more often characterized in maternal than paternal terms. Guerric urged a wider application of maternal imagery among his monks. "Brethren," he said to them on one occasion, "this name of mother is not restricted to prelates . . . [I]t is shared by you too who do God's will. Yes, you too are mothers of the Child who has been born for you and in you . . . Keep

---

57. Origen, *Song of Songs*, 38–39.
58. Augustine, *Sermons on the Liturgical Seasons*, 31.
59. Maximus the Confessor, *Ambiguorum Liber*, 1084.
60. Doyle, *Bringing Forth Christ*, viii.
61. "'Who are my mother and my brothers?' And looking about at those who sat around him, [Jesus] said, 'Here are my mother and my brothers! For whoever does the will of God, he is my brother and sister and mother.'"
62. "A woman in the crowd raised her voice and said to [Jesus], 'Blessed the womb that bore you and the breasts at which you nursed!' But he said, 'Blessed rather are those who hear the word of God and keep it!'"
63. Guerric, *Liturgical Sermons*, xxxvii.

watch, then, holy mother, keep watch in your care for the new-born child until Christ is formed in you who was born for you."[64]

Every Christian a Mother of Christ

At the beginning of the thirteenth century St. Francis of Assisi could say, "We are mothers when we carry [Jesus] in our heart and body through love and pure and sincere conscience, ... giv[ing] birth to him through his holy manner of working which should shine before others as an example."[65] In his *Bringing Forth Christ: Five Feasts of the Child Jesus*,[66] an extended commentary on the question put to his disciples by Jesus ("Who is my mother?"), St. Bonaventure develops this idea further. "By the grace of the Holy Spirit and the power of the Most High," he writes in the prologue to that work, "a soul dedicated to God [can] spiritually conceive the holy Word of God and only-begotten Son of the Father, give birth to him, name him, seek and adore him, and finally, according to the law of Moses, joyfully present him in the Temple to God the Father."[67] Like Guerric and the mystic Beguine, Hadewijch (his thirteenth-century contemporary), Bonaventure can speak of "the heavenly Father[,] by a divine seed, as it were, [impregnating] the soul and [making] it fruitful."[68] The Son of God, who is thereby spiritually conceived, is born in the soul when, "after good advice, due thought and prayer for God's protection, we put into practice our resolution to lead a more perfect life."[69]

St. Bonaventure's "spiritual motherhood" became a "doctrine concerning the mystical birth of God's Word in the soul, and the vocation of every Christian to become a mother of Christ."[70] It was based, says Doyle, on the conviction that "there is a maternal relationship with Christ in our spiritual lives, a most intimate union between Christ and the soul, represented symbolically as the relationship between a mother and the baby conceived in her womb."[71]

---

64. Guerric, *Liturgical Sermons*, 52.
65. Armstrong and Brady, *Francis and Clare*, 63.
66. Excerpts from which are found in appendix 3.
67. Doyle, *Bringing Forth Christ*, 2.
68. Doyle, *Bringing Forth Christ*, 3.
69. Doyle, *Bringing Forth Christ*, 7.
70. Doyle, *Bringing Forth Christ*, iii.
71. Doyle, *Bringing Forth Christ*, viii.

APPENDIX 2: BRINGING FORTH JESUS AS IMITATIO MARIAE

Francis de Sales and *Imitatio Mariae*

This tradition, known as *Imitatio Mariae* (Imitation of Mary), continued strong in Dominican circles during the fourteenth century and was revived and flourished in the period of the Counter-Reformation. It was, however, to receive its definitive expression in the mystical theology of St. Francis de Sales, whose life and work bridged the end of the sixteenth and the beginning of the seventeenth century. The founder of a religious congregation called "Visitation of Holy Mary," de Sales developed his thinking on this subject in letters written to its superior, his close associate, Jane de Chantel. Typical is the following, found in one such letter: "Our souls must give birth, not outside themselves but inside themselves, to the sweetest, gentlest, and most beautiful male child imaginable. It is Jesus whom we must bring to birth and produce in ourselves. You are pregnant with him, my dear sister, and blessed be God who is his Father."[72]

According to Wendy Wright, who has written about the Salesian understanding of the Christian life under the metaphor of "birthing Jesus," de Sales believed that "the ultimate meaning of human life is to be found in bringing Jesus into the world."[73] In de Sales's view as Wright describes it, "the divine enters history and takes flesh through the medium of the human person," and "this can happen at any point in history." "The individual, like the Virgin Mary," she says, "can be a mother of God [by] being receptive to the Spirit of God which hovers in anticipation around the human soul, desiring to enter it, to cause it to conceive and then give birth, making divine life present in the world."

The resulting maternal symbolism, which is foundational to the Salesian conception of the Christian life, is not only "descriptive of the mystical process of union with the design," says Wright, "but is the means to union itself, the medium through which one becomes a mother of God."[74] For de Sales, *Imitatio Mariae* is thus no longer a metaphor but a symbol, initiating a process of internal and structural change which is a "becoming Mary," "becoming a mother of God, allowing the Word of God to become incarnate, to enter one's most intimate self, to change that self from the inside and then birth Jesus (the Word) through the flesh."[75]

---

72. Wright, "Birthing Jesus," 23.
73. Wright, "Birthing Jesus," 23.
74. Wright, "Birthing Jesus," 24.
75. Wright, "Birthing Jesus," 32–33.

APPENDIX 2: BRINGING FORTH JESUS AS IMITATIO MARIAE

To describe this, as Wright points out, de Sales employed language of descent rather than ascent, of dwelling and indwelling rather than journeying. In so doing, he "affirms that the location of union with God is not beyond but within human history" and "that God did not come to remove the reality of the human situation but to fill it with divine presence":[76] "The word as symbol which has made the individual 'pregnant' contains within itself the embryo of the transformation that he or she must gestate and into which he or she is invited to grow . . . The invitation is to further internalization, new 'conception,' so that rebirth might become reality and be enfleshed once again."[77]

For her part, Mary as symbol is the Church at prayer, hearing the Word, allowing it

> to enter, gestate, transform, and be born in her, giving new life to the world, allowing Jesus to live.[78] She is the diagram of the formative process that makes the transformation possible. She bespeaks the openness of womb and ear to seed and word. She is the dwelling place of the incarnate God. She is a statement of the radically incarnational mysticism that affirms the intimate union of the divine and human in history and flesh and the ever-present moment . . . She is what the Christian mystical tradition proclaims all persons are and must become. To imitate her is to let Jesus live, to become a mother of God.[79]

Undergirding the Salesian understanding of the Christian life, Wright concludes, are twin pillars. On the one hand, there is "the theological assertion of the Incarnation, a divine/human reality that, as the formative tradition of Christian prayer insists, is an ongoing and unfolding event." On the other, we can discern "the symbol of the Virgin Mary whose own conception, gestation, and birthing of the divine seed is a paradigm for the Church and the individual Christian, called like her to spiritual motherhood."[80]

Prominent twentieth-century exponents of the *Imitatio Mariae* include George A. Maloney, whose book *Mary: The Womb of God* (1976) takes its title from the famous phrase of Ireneaus, and the English Roman Catholic laywoman Caryll Houselander, author of *The Reed of God* (1944)

---

76. Wright, "Birthing Jesus," 30.
77. Wright, "Birthing Jesus," 40.
78. The Salesian motto was "Live Jesus!"
79. Wright, "Birthing Jesus," 40–41.
80. Wright, "Birthing Jesus," 40.

APPENDIX 2: BRINGING FORTH JESUS AS IMITATIO MARIAE

and *The Mother of Christ* (1978). In the former of those works, Houselander sums up the tradition as follows: "Each saint has his special work: one person's work. But our Lady had to include in her vocation, in her life's work, the essential thing that was to be hidden in every other vocation, in every life . . . The one thing that she did and does is the one thing that we all have to do, namely, to bear Christ into the world."[81]

---

81. Houselander, *Reed of God*, xii.

Appendix 3

From *Bringing Forth Christ: Five Feasts of the Child Jesus* by St. Bonaventure[82]

The First Feast[83]: How Christ Jesus, the Son of God, May Be Conceived Spiritually by a Devout Soul

1. OUR UNDERSTANDING HAS to be purified by the waters of sorrow, our heart inflamed and raised on high by the gentle fire of love. Then by fervent meditation and prayerful thought we can undertake our first consideration: How it is that the blessed Son of God, Christ Jesus, may be conceived spiritually in a devout soul.

Once a devout soul has been touched or moved by the hope of heavenly bliss, the fear of eternal punishment or the weariness of living long in this vale of tears [Ps 83:7], it is visited by fresh inspirations, set alight with holy desires and taken up with godly thoughts. When at length it has rejected and despised previous imperfections and former desires for worldly things, and has resolved to lead a new life by the gracious kindness of the

---

82. First edition. Copyright © SLG Press, 1984. Reproduced by permission of the Convent of the Incarnation, Oxford, England.

83. Pages 3–6. The Feast of the Annunciation, March 25. The other four are the feasts of the Nativity (December 25, see below), the Holy Name of Jesus (January 2), the Epiphany (January 6), and the Presentation (February 2).

APPENDIX 3: BRINGING FORTH CHRIST: FIVE FEASTS OF THE CHILD JESUS

Father of lights from whom is every good endowment and every perfect gift [Jas 1:17], it conceives mystically by the gift of grace.

What is happening here? It is nothing other than the heavenly Father by a divine seed, as it were, impregnating the soul and making it fruitful. The power of the Most High comes upon the soul and overshadows it [Luke 1:35] with a heavenly coolness which tempers the desires of the flesh and gives help and strength to the eyes of the spirit.

2. It is a joyous conception which leads to such contempt of the world and to such longing for heavenly works and the things of God. No matter how fleetingly up to this point, even in the midst of distress, the things of the spirit have been tasted, the things of the flesh lose their savor.

Now, with Mary, the soul begins to climb the hill country [Luke 1:39] because after this conception earthly things lose their attraction, and the soul longs for heavenly and eternal things. The soul begins to flee the company of those with minds set on earthly things [Phil 3:19] and desires the friendship of those with hearts set on heavenly things. It begins to take care of Elizabeth, that is, to look to those who are enlightened by divine wisdom and ardently inflamed by love.

There is an important point to keep in mind because it applies to many people: the further one withdraws from the world, the closer becomes one's friendship with good people. And it follows that the more the company of ungodly people loses its attraction, the more the company of saintly and spiritual people inspires the heart with radiant delight. As St. Gregory says, "Anyone who keeps close to a holy man discovers that by seeing him often, listening to his words and witnessing his exemplary behavior, he is set on fire with love of the truth, keeps away from the darkness of sin and is inflamed by the love of divine light." And St. Isidore writes: "Seek the company of good people. If you share their company, you will also share their virtue."

The faithful soul should consider well how pure, holy and devout was the conversation of the saints, how godly and salutary their counsel, how admirable their holiness, and all they achieved to their mutual benefit, as they inspired one another by word and example towards greater virtue.

3. Devout soul, that is also what you should do when you realize that you have, by the Holy Spirit, conceived a new longing for the life of grace. Avoid the company of the wicked, go up into the hill country with Mary, seek the advice of spiritual people, strive to follow in the footsteps of the saints, reflect upon the teaching of holy people and also upon their actions

APPENDIX 3: BRINGING FORTH CHRIST: FIVE FEASTS OF THE CHILD JESUS

and example. Keep clear of the poisonous counsels of the wicked who always try to distort new desires inspired by the Holy Spirit and want to hinder them and never cease to tear them to shreds.

Often under the guise of holiness they infect the soul with the contagion of an insidious cowardice. They say such things as: What you have begun is beyond you; what you are taking on is far too difficult; what you are doing is too much of a burden. Your strength is not up to it, you do not have the ability to do it. Your mind will get confused, your eyesight will be destroyed, you will develop all kinds of illnesses: consumption, paralysis, stones in the kidneys, dizziness in the head, dulling of the senses, clouding of the mind and loss of faculties. All these terrible things will happen to you if you do not abandon what you have started and take greater care of your health. Such practices do not become your position, they harm your honor and good name.'

You notice then how someone can masquerade as a master of discipline and a medical doctor, who does not even know how to keep his own life in order or cure the sickness of his own mind! How sad it is that the cursed advice of the worldly-minded has frequently ruined so many people and killed the Son of God conceived in them by the Holy Spirit. This is that damnable and deadly medicine, the devil's counsel, which hinders spiritual conception in so many souls, and kills and destroys in many others what had been conceived by a firm decision or a vow.

4. There are others who seem to be good, religious people, and perhaps they are, but who, I say it with respect, are far too timid. They forget that the hand of the Lord is not yet shortened that it cannot save [Isa 59:1], nor do they remember that the kindness of the Most High has not yet run out, that he wants to help us and has the power to do so. They have a zeal for God but it is not enlightened [Rom 10:2]. Out of compassion for physical suffering or perhaps from fear of natural weakness, they dissuade others from the pursuit of perfection. That is their reaction when they see others achieving successfully that which they themselves had judged to be good and holy, but upon which they did not have the courage to embark. They discourage others from anything that goes beyond the common average and they destroy the salutary counsels which come from God's inspiration. And the more authentic these counsels are in the light of their experience, the more dangerous they find them to be.

5. Sometimes through the cunning of the ancient enemy they slyly suggest: "If you take on such and such practices of piety, people will say

you are holy, good, devout and religious. And because you have not yet acquired the virtues which others think you have, you will be judged guilty in the sight of the Supreme Judge who knows in all their horror your great and terrible sins. You will forfeit the merits of your good works, and you will be judged a liar and a hypocrite." Such practices of piety, they maintain, are only for those who have not sinned gravely and have kept to a chaste and holy life, who gave up everything for God and have remained faithful to him all their lives.

6. Beloved soul dedicated to God; keep clear of people like that. Go up into the hill country [Luke 1:39] with Mary. St. Paul did not live a sinless life. Yet he had not been in God's service for any length of time, when he was taken up into the third heaven and contemplated God face to face [2 Cor 12:2–4]. St. Mary Magdalene had been full of pride and ambition, totally intent on worldly vanities and ensnared by the pleasures of the flesh. Yet not long after her conversion she sat among the holy Apostles at the feet of Jesus and listened attentively to the saving doctrine of perfection. She was found worthy to be the first to see the Lord shortly after his resurrection and she proclaimed steadfastly to the others that he was risen from the dead [Luke 7:37–47; 8:2; John 20:1–2].

God shows no partiality [Acts 10:34]. He does not take account of nobility of birth, length of time in his service or the number of our good works. What counts with God is a devout soul's increased fervor and more ardent love. He does not consider how you once behaved, but what you have now begun to be. You see therefore how gravely blameworthy the advice of such would be, did ignorance not excuse it, though it cannot be condoned.

7. If then you cannot be saved through innocence, strive for salvation by penance. If you cannot be a Catherine or a Cecilia, do not be ashamed to be a Mary Magdalene or a Mary of Egypt. If you recognize that you have conceived God's most dear Son by a sacred resolve to strive for perfection, then keep away from the deadly poison I have just mentioned and, like a woman in labor, hasten with desire and longing towards a happy delivery.

The Second Feast[84]: How the Son of God Is Born Spiritually in a Devout Soul

1. SECONDLY, LET US CONSIDER and mark well how the blessed the Son of God, already conceived spiritually, is born spiritually in the soul. He is born

---

84. Pages 7–8. The Feast of the Nativity (December 25).

APPENDIX 3: BRINGING FORTH CHRIST: FIVE FEASTS OF THE CHILD JESUS

when, after good advice, through thought and prayer for God's protection, we put into practice our resolution to lead a more perfect life. He is born when the soul begins to do that which it long had in mind but was afraid to undertake through fear of its own weakness. The angels rejoice at this most blessed birth, they glorify God and announce peace [Luke 2:13].

They announce peace because peace is restored to the soul by the practice of the virtues that it long had in mind. God's peace cannot be firmly established in the soul while the spirit and flesh are at war with each other [Gal 5:7]; when the spirit longs for solitude and the flesh crazes to be with the crowd; when the spirit delights in Christ and the flesh is allured by the world; when the spirit seeks the serenity of contemplation in God and the flesh desires positions of honor in the world.

On the other hand, when the flesh is subjected to the spirit, that is, once good works are put into practice—which for so long the flesh had hindered—peace is surely restored to the soul. How happy a birth which brings such rejoicing to men and angels! How lovely and delightful it would be if we always did what is best for us. But our foolishness prevents it. Once we rid ourselves of our foolishness, human nature recognizes what is native to it. In this birth, we experience the truth of that gospel saying: "Take my yoke upon you, and learn from me, for I am gentle and lowly and heart, and you will find rest for your soul. For my yoke is easy and my burden is light" (Matt 11:29–30).

2. Devout Soul, if this happy birth brings you delights: you should remember that you must be like Mary. The name "Mary" means "bitter sea," "one who enlightens," and "one who rules." First you must be a "bitter sea" of tears of sorrow, weeping bitterly for the sins you have committed, lamenting deeply the good you have left undone, and reproach yourself unceasingly for the time you let slip by and lost. Second, you must be "one who enlightens" by speaking words of edification, practicing virtue and teaching others untiringly to do good. Third, you must be "one who rules," that is, be master of your senses, of carnal passion and of all your actions. In this way, all your actions will be in conformity with right reason, and in all that you do, you will seek and long for God's praise and glory, your neighbor's edification and your own salvation.

3. How blessed is such a "Mary" who weeps over sins committed, shines resplendently with virtue and has complete mastery over all carnal desires. Jesus Christ does not disdain to be born spiritually and joyfully, without pain and sorrow, from a "Mary" like this.

Once this birth has taken place, the devout soul knows and tastes how good the Lord Jesus is [Ps 34:9]. And in truth we find how good he is when we nourish him with our prayers, bathe him in the waters of our warm and loving tears, wrap him in the spotless swaddling clothes of our desires, carry him in an embrace of holy love, kiss him repeatedly with heartfelt longing and cherish him in the bosom of our innermost heart. That is how this Child is born spiritually in a devout soul.

Bibliography

Allison, Dale C. Jr. *The End of the Ages Has Come: An Early Interpretation of the Passion and Resurrection of Jesus*. Philadelphia: Fortress. 1985.
Ambrose. "Joseph." In *Saint Ambrose: Seven Exegetical Works*, edited by Bernard M. Peebles and translated by Michael P. McHugh, 187–240. Washington, DC: Catholic University Press, 1972.
Anselm. *Prayers and Meditations of St. Anselm with the Proslogion*. Translated by Benedicta Ward. New York: Penguin, 1973.
Armstrong, R. J., and I. Brady, eds. *Francis and Clare: The Complete Works*. Mahwah, NJ: Paulist, 1986.
Augustine of Hippo. *Homilies on the Gospel of John, 1–40*. In *The Works of Saint Augustine*, edited by Allan D. Fitzgerald and translated by Edmund Hill. Hyde Park, NY: New City, 2009.
———. *Sermons on the Liturgical Seasons*. Translated by Mary Sarah Muldowney. Washington, DC: Catholic University of America Press, 1959.
Barrett, C. K. *A Commentary on the First Epistle to the Corinthians*. New York: Bloomsbury, 1968.
Baumgarten, Joseph, and Mansoor, Menahem. "Studies in the New *Hodayot* [Thanksgiving Hymns]–II." In *Journal of Biblical Literature* 74 (1955) 188–95.
Beare, A. W. *A Commentary on the Epistle to the Philippians*. New York: Bloomsbury. 1959.
Bennett, Thomas Andrew. *Labor of God: The Agony of the Cross as the Birth of the Church*. Waco, TX: Baylor University Press, 2017.
Bertram, George. "*Odin/odino*." In *Theological Dictionary of the New Testament*, edited by Gerhard Friedrich and Geoffrey Bromiley, 9:667–74. Grand Rapids: Eerdmans, 1974.
Black, Matthew. *Romans*. Grand Rapids: Eerdmans, 1973.
Blumenfeld-Kosinski, Renate, ed. and transl. *The Writings of Marguerite of Oingt, Medieval Prioress and Mystic*. Newburyport, MA: Focus, 1990.
Boice, James. *Foundations of the Christian Faith*. Downers Grove, IL: InterVarsity, 1986.
Bonhoeffer, Dietrich. *Ethics*. London: SCM, 1955.

Bright, John. *The Kingdom of God: The Biblical Concept and Its Meaning for the Church.* Nashville: Abingdon, 1953.
Brodie, Thomas L. *The Gospel according to John: A Literary and Theological Commentary.* New York: Oxford University Press, 1993.
Brown, Raymond. *The Gospel according to John (I-XII).* New York: Doubleday, 1966.
———. *The Gospel according to John (XIII-XXI).* New Haven: Yale University Press, 1970.
Catechism of the Catholic Church. Liguori, MD: Liguori, 1994.
Cerny, Ladislov. *The Day of Yahweh and Some Relevant Problems.* Prague, 1948.
Chappuis, Jean-Marc. "Jesus and the Samaritan Woman: The Variable Geometry of Communication." In *The Ecumenical Review* 34:1 (January 1982) 8–34.
Clement of Alexandria. *The Instructor.* Translated by William Wilson. Buffalo, NY: Christian Literature, 1885.
Colledge, Edmund, and James Walsh, eds. and transls. *Julian of Norwich, Showings.* Mahwah, NJ: Paulist, 1978.
Congar, Yves. *The Wide World My Parish: Salvation and Its Problems.* Baltimore: Helicon, 1961.
Cullmann, Oscar. *The Early Church.* London: SCM, 1956.
De Waal, Esther. *Living with Contradiction: An Introduction to Benedictine Spirituality.* Harrisburg, PA: Morehouse, 1989.
Dix, Gregory. *The Image and Likeness of God.* New York: Morehouse-Gorham, 1954.
Donne, John. "Death's Duel, or, A Consolation to the Soul, Against the Dying Life and Living Death of the Body." In *The Showing Forth of Christ: Sermons of John Donne,* edited by Edmund Fuller, 210–28. New York: Harper & Row, 1964.
———. "The Showing Forth of Christ: A Christmas Sermon." In *The Showing Forth of Christ: Sermons of John Donne,* edited by Edmund Fuller, 76–88. New York: Harper & Row, 1964.
Doyle, Eric, ed. and transl. *Bringing Forth Christ: Five Feasts of the Christ Child by St. Bonaventure.* 1st ed. Oxford: SLG, 1984.
Dunn, James D. J. *Romans 1–8.* Grand Rapids: Zondervan, 1988.
Dupont-Sommer, A. *The Essene Writings from Qumran.* Cleveland: World, 1961.
Feuillet, Andre. *Johannine Studies.* Staten Island, NY: Alba House, 1965.
Fitzmyer, Joseph. "The Letter to the Galatians." In *The Jerome Biblical Commentary,* edited by Raymond E. Brown et al., 2:236–46. Englewood Cliffs, NJ: Prentice-Hall, 1968.
Gabriel of St. Mary Magdalene. *Divine Intimacy: Meditations on the Interior Life for Every Day of the Year.* New York: Desclee, 1963.
Gage, W. A. *The Gospel of Genesis.* Winona Lake, IL: Carpenter Books, 1984.
Gaster, Moses. *The Samaritans: Their History, Doctrines, and Literature.* London: Humphrey Milford, 1925.
Glasson, T. Francis. *Moses in the Fourth Gospel.* London: SCM, 1963.
Guerric of Igny. *Liturgical Sermons.* Spencer, MA: Cistercian Publications, 1970.
Hall, Francis J. *Creation and Man.* New York: Longmans, Green, 1912.
Hanson, Anthony T. *Jesus Christ in the Old Testament.* London: SPCK, 1965.
Henry, Matthew, et al., eds. *The Bethany Parallel Commentary on the New Testament.* Ada, MI: Baker, 1983.
Hoskyns, Edwyn. *The Fourth Gospel.* London: Faber and Faber, 1947.
Houselander, Caryll. *The Mother of Christ.* London: Sheed and Ward, 1978.
———. *The Passion of the Infant Christ.* New York: Sheed and Ward, 1949.
———. *The Reed of God.* New York: Sheed and Ward, 1944.

Ignatius. "Epistle to the Romans." In *The Apostolic Fathers*, edited by J. B. Lightfoot and J. R. Harmer, 149–53. 1891. Reprint, Grand Rapids: Baker, 1984.
Johnson, Marshall D. *The Purpose of the Biblical Genealogies, with Special Reference to the Setting of the Genealogies of Jesus*. Cambridge: Cambridge University Press, 1969.
Kaufmann, Walter, ed. *Basic Writings of Nietzsche*. New York: Modern Library, 1968.
Keil, C. F., and Franz Delitzsch. *The Pentateuch*. 1864. Reprint, Grand Rapids: Eerdmans, 1973.
Keller, Timothy. *Walking with God through Pain and Suffering*. New York: Dutton, 2013.
Kenneth, Brother, ed. *From the Fathers to the Churches: Daily Spiritual Readings*. London: Collins, 1983.
Klausner, Joseph. *The Messianic Idea in Israel from Its Beginning to the Completion of the Mishnah*. New York: MacMillan, 1955.
LeFrois, Bernard J. *The Woman Clothed with the Sun (Apocalypse 12): Individual or Collective? (An Exegetical Study)*. Rome: Orbis Catholicus, 1954.
Leeming, Bernard. *Principles of Sacramental Theology*. Westminster, MD: Newman, 1956.
Lewis, C. S. *A Grief Observed*. New York: Seabury, 1961.
———. *The Problem of Pain*. New York: MacMillan, 1940.
Linders, Barnabus. *The Gospel of John*. Grand Rapids: Eerdmans, 1972.
Lloyd-Jones, Gareth. *The Bones of Joseph: From the Ancient Texts to the Modern Church*. Grand Rapids: Eerdmans, 1997.
MacDonald, John. *The Theology of the Samaritans*. London: SCM, 1964.
Maloney, George. *Mary: The Womb of God*. Denville, NJ: Dimension, 1978.
Marsh, John. *Saint John*. Philadelphia: Westminster, 1968.
Martin, Ralph. *Philippians*. Grand Rapids: Eerdmans, 1976.
Mascall, E. L. *Christ, the Christian, and the Church: A Study of the Incarnation and Its Consequences*. London: Longmans, Green, 1946.
Maximus the Confessor. *Ambiguorum Liber*. Paris: Imprimarie Catholique, n. d.
Meeks, Wayne A. *The Prophet-King: Moses Traditions and the Johannine Christology*. Leiden: E. J. Brill, 1967.
Michel, Otto. "*Oikos*." In *Theological Dictionary of the New Testament*, edited by Gerhard Friedrich and Geoffrey W. Bromiley, 5:136–44. Grand Rapids: Eerdmans, 1967.
Montgomery, James A. *The Samaritans: The Earliest Jewish Sect*. New York: KTAV, 1907.
Mowinckel, Sigmund. *He That Cometh*. Oxford: Basil Blackwell, 1959.
Nouwen, Henri J. M. *The Wounded Healer: Ministry in Contemporary Society*. Garden City, NJ: Doubleday, 1972.
Odeberg, Hugo. *The Fourth Gospel, Interpreted in Relation to Contemporaneous Religious Currents in Palestine and the Hellenistic-Oriental World*. Amsterdam: B. R. Gruner, 1968.
Origen, *The Song of Songs: Commentary and Homilies*. Mahwah, NJ: Paulist, 1957.
Pamment, Margaret. "John 3:5, Unless One Is Born of Water and Spirit, He Cannot Enter the Kingdom of Heaven." In *Novum Testamentum* 25:2 (1983) 189–90.
Plummer, Alfred. *The Gospel according to St. Mark*. Cambridge: Cambridge University Press, 1938.
Rice, Richard. *Suffering and the Search for Meaning: Contemporary Responses to the Problem of Pain*. Downers Grove, IL: IVP Academic, 2014.
Robinson, H. Wheeler. *Suffering Human and Divine*. New York: MacMillan, 1939.
Rowley, H. H. *The Relevance of Apocalyptic: A Study of Jewish and Christian Apocalypses from Daniel to the Revelation*. New York: Association, 1944.

Sanders, J. N. *A Commentary on the Gospel According to St. John*. New York: Bloomsbury, 1968.
Sasson, Jack M. *Jonah*. New York: Doubleday, 1990.
Schillebeekx, Edward. *Christ the Sacrament of the Encounter with God*. London: Sheed and Ward, 1963.
Schnackenburg, Rudolph. *The Gospel According to St. John*. Vol. 1. Translated by Kevin Smyth. New York: Herder and Herder, 1968.
———. *The Gospel According to St. John*. Vol. 3. Translated by David Smith and G. A. Kon. New York: Herder and Herder, 1982.
Tillich, Paul. *The Protestant Era*. Translated by James Luther Adams. Chicago: University of Chicago Press, 1957.
Vawter, Bruce. *On Genesis: A New Reading*. Garden City, NY: Doubleday, 1977.
Wagner, Siegfried. "*Banah*." In *Theological Dictionary of the Old Testament*, edited by G. Johannes Botterweck and Helmer Ringgren, 2:166–81. Grand Rapids: Eerdmans, 1975.
Wenham, Gordon J. *Genesis 16–50*. Grand Rapids: Zondervan, 1994.
Westermann, Claus. *Genesis 1–11: A Commentary*. Translated by John J. Scullion. Minneapolis: Augsburg, 1984.
———. *Genesis 37–50: A Commentary*. Translated by John J. Scullion. Minneapolis: Augsburg, 1986.
Witherington, Ben, III. "The Waters of Birth: John 3:5 and 1 John 5:6–8." In *New Testament Studies* 35 (1989) 155–60.
Wolff, H. H. *Joel and Amos*. Philadelphia: Fortress, 1977.
Wright, Wendy. "Birthing Jesus: A Salesian Understanding of the Christian Life." In *Studia Mystica* 13:1 (Spring 1990) 23–44.

Scripture Index

n = footnote
LXX = Septuagint

Genesis

1:1	74n2
1:2	54, 74
1:3	23, 56, 73
1:6	73, 74n3
1:8	74n3
1:9	74n3
1:10	74n3
1:11	73
1:14	73
1:20	73
1:24	73
1:26–30	3n4
1:26–27	2
1:26	3, 4, 73
1:27	3
1:28	6, 15, 58
2:1–3	74
2:4	110
2:5–23	3n4
2:5–7	2
2:7	3, 54, 76, 87
2:18	4, 48, 50
2:21–23	2
2:21–22	45, 48
2:21	84
2:23	55, 84
2:24	3, 9
3:5	4
3:15	1, 5
3:16	7, 8
3:17–19	9, 16
3:20	44
4:1	59
4:8–16	45n24
4:10–11	77
4:10	17n23, 44
4:11	16
4:15–16	17n24
4:15	17
4:25	44
5:1	81, 110
6:5–13	78
6:9	81, 110
8:21	80
10:1	81, 110
10:32	110
11:10	81, 110
11:27	81, 110
12:1	24
12:2	110
12:3	110

SCRIPTURE INDEX

Genesis *(continued)*

12:6–7	95n6
12:7	6
13:14	24
15:1–4	24
15:5	6, 24
15:6	24
17:1	24
17:17	24
18:1	24
18:12	24
21:2	24
22:1	24
29:1–14	96
29:1–2	105
29:6	105
29:7	105
29:9	105
29:10	105
29:18	105
29:19–20	105
29:31	105
30:1	49
30:24	105n46
33:18–19	94
35:16–19	26
35:16–18	40
35:18	105
35:19	43
36:1	110
37:2	100, 110
37:3	104
37:5–11	100, 102
37:11	100
37:12–14	104
37:18–20	100
37:28	104
37:31–33	104
37:33	100
39:2–3	101
39:21	101
39:23	101
40:1–13	99
40:8	101
40:9–15	101
40:20–21	101
41:1–8	99
41:15	101
41:25	99
41:38	99
41:53–57	110
45:1–3	104n42
45:16–20	100
46:28	100
48:21–22	94
49:22	109
49:25	112
50:2	111
50:20	38
50:24–25	102
50:24	94
50:25	94
50:26	111

Exodus

1:19	88
2:16–22	96
2:23–25	20
3:7–9	20
3:7	58
4:22	34
7:14—12:32	21
7:14–24	53
8:1–7	53
8:16–19	53
8:20–24	53
9:13–26	52
10:12–20	52
10:21–23	53
12:7	53
12:12–13	53
12:29–30	53
12:41	53
13:2	20
13:11–16	20
13:19	94, 102
13:21–22	94n5
13:21	53
14:10	53
14:21–31	53
14:21–29	21
14:21–22	53

SCRIPTURE INDEX

15:1–18	28
15:13–16	28
19:4–6	21
19:4	102
19:6	99
28:32	40

Numbers

22:12	38

Deuteronomy

2:25	28
18:15	97
23:5	38
32:11	41
32:18	20, 41
33:13–16	110
33:16	100n32

Joshua

24:32	95, 102

Ruth

4:11–12	49

1 Samuel

16:13	23

2 Samuel

2:4	23
5:3	23
7:10	107n49
7:11–13	49
7:14	56

Nehemiah

13:2	38

Job

1:21	62
1:26	81
19:25–27	46
42:1–6	46

Psalms

2:7	23, 55
17:5 (LXX)	36
17:6 (LXX)	36n8
18:5–6	37
18:5	36n8
18:16	22
30:5	39
32:6	22
34:9	124
41:1	38
41:3	38
42:7	22
48:4–6	28
48:6	ix, 27
69:1–2	22
69:14–15	22
72:6	88
78:67	111n53
80:1	111
80:8	111
81:5	111n53
83:7	119
88:3	21
88:4	21
88:5	21
88:6–7	21
88:15–17	21
89:26–28	23
90:2	75
91:4	41
105:6	103
105:17–22	103
110:3	23, 55
114:3 (LXX)	36
116:3	36n8, 37
116:15	38
122:3	48
139:13	77
139:15	77, 81

Proverbs

3:11–12	51
30:18–19	96
30:20	96

Ecclesiastes

11:4	109
11:5	106
11:6	109

Song of Songs

5:2–8	96n14

Isaiah

2:10–12	77
9:6	30n24
13:4–13	77
13:8	27, 28
21:1–4	29
21:3	xiii, 27
26:16–18	30
26:17	27
42:14	27, 41
45:9–10	30
48:10	x
49:15	41
52:1–2	49
53:3	34
54:5	20
59:1	121
61:3	39
62:4–5	49
65:17	56, 73
66:7–9	30
66:14	107n49

Jeremiah

4:31	27
6:22–24	29
6:24	xiii, 27
8:21	29
10:10	77
13:21	27
22:23	27
30:6	xiii, 27
31:15	27
49:24	27
50:43	27

Ezekiel

37:1–2	76
37:1	106
37:4–6	106
37:6	77
37:7	106
37:8	106
37:10	109
37:11–14	106

Daniel

7:13	84
9:27	31
12:1–2	82
12:4	31

Hosea

11:1	34, 102n38
13:13	20n4, 27, 30
14:6	88

Joel

2:25	52n11
2:28–31	52
2:32	53

Amos

5:18	83
8:8–9	77

Obadiah

18	98

Jonah

2:1	22
2:2	22n8
2:3	22
2:5–6	22

Micah

4:8–10	29
5:2	26, 27
5:3	26

Nahum

1:5–6	77

Zephaniah

1:14–15	83

Zechariah

8:13	38
14:4–5	77

2 Maccabees

7:22	106n47

Matthew

1:1	16
1:1–17	24n12
2:13–15	34
2:16	26
2:18	27
6:10	79
7:13	11
7:17–20	11
7:23	11
7:24	11
9:36	41
11:29–30	123
12:40	22n8, 79
13:31–32	76
14:14	41
15:32	41
16:16	19
18:27	41
20:34	41
23:27	111n55
24:3–51	32
24:3	18
24:6–7	18
24:8	18, 47, 57
24:15	31
24:21	57
24:27	86
27:46	43
27:50–52	77
27:51	39n13
27:52	45
27:52–53	76
27:53	46
27:55–56	39
27:61	39
28:1–10	39
28:1–2	77

Mark

1:41	41
2:11	38
3:3–37	32
3:32–35	72
3:33–34	114
4:17	83
4:26–29	109
4:30–32	109
6:34	41
8:2	41
8:31	68
9:19	67
9:22	41
9:31	68
10:34	68
11:18	104
12:1–11	104
12:6	104
12:8	104
12:27	111n55
13:19	57, 83
13:24	83

Mark *(continued)*

13:32	84
15:34	43
15:40–41	39, 43
15:47	39
16:1–9	39

Luke

1:28	25
1:31	25, 33, 57
1:35	25, 57
1:38	25, 105
1:39	120, 122
1:42	33
2:13–14	56
2:13	123
2:35	27, 45
3:21–22	56
3:22	34
3:23–36	6
3:23	16
7:13	41
7:37–47	122
8:2	122
9:23	69
10:33	41, 104n43
11:28	114
12:50	56
13:34	41
15:20	41
21:10–36	32
21:23	57
23:27–29	41
23:34	12, 85
23:46	85
23:47	44
23:49	39
23:55–56	39
24:1–8	39
24:36	54

John

1:1	4, 25
1:3	75
1:14	23, 25, 76
1:17	100
1:18	4, 23, 25
1:25	97
1:40–42	xv
1:45	xv
1:46	xv
3:3	61, 62
3:4	62
3:5	33, 65n13
3:6	61, 64, 65
3:8	109
3:16	4, 23
3:18	23
3:28–29	93
3:30	68
4:5	94
4:6	94, 95, 109n52
4:7	95
4:8	94, 95, 108
4:9	104n43
4:10	105
4:12	96, 105
4:16–18	104n43
4:16	96
4:17–18	96
4:19	97
4:21	105
4:22	97, 107
4:25–26	104
4:25	97
4:26	107
4:27	107
4:28	107
4:29	108
4:31	108
4:34	108
4:35–38	108
4:39	112
4:41	112
4:42	112
5:18	100
5:28–29	111n55
5:29	89
5:46	100
6:1–11	100
6:14	97, 99

SCRIPTURE INDEX

6:15	100	1:14–15	52
6:32	100n33	1:14	54
7:1	100	1:15	54
7:3–5	100	1:26	54
7:40	97	2:1–4	48, 51
8:12	86	2:1–3	57
8:39–59	100	2:2	54
8:39–47	6n9	2:11	48
8:48	104n43	2:17–20	52
8:49	104n43	2:17	82
10:31–39	100	2:21	53
11:33	41	2:22–24	36
11:35	41	2:23–24	33
11:38–39	41	2:23	44
11:43–44	41	2:24	34, 40, 56, 81n13
11:45–53	100	2:26	44
12:24	69, 76, 109	2:36	33
12:46	23	3:13	34
13:34	48	3:26	34
14:2	100	4:3	54
14:19	51	4:27	34
14:20	14, 72	4:30	34
14:23	52	5:18	54
15:1	111n54	5:33	54
15:4	68	5:40	54
16:20–22	83	5:41	54
16:20	39	6:15	85
16:21	8, 13, 54, 69, 91	7:55	84
17:1	13	7:56	12, 84
19:19	27	7:59–60	85
19:25	27, 39	7:60	12
19:26–27	44	8:1	54
19:28	43	8:55	51n9
19:29	43	9:2	85
19:30	43	9:3–6	85
19:34	45	9:5	12
20:1–2	39, 122	9:31	54
20:11–18	39	10:34	122
20:17	27n17	11:19	83
20:22	48	13:33–34	56
21:1–13	100	14:22	65
		16:26	39n13
		17:28	63
		26:14	14

Acts

1:3	27n17
1:12–13	54

SCRIPTURE INDEX

Romans

1:4	34
2:9	83
4:19	68n21
5:3–4	14
6:3–4	61
6:5	69
8:9	51, 87
8:11	87
8:17	81
8:18	81
8:19	80, 82
8:21	80, 82n13
8:22	73, 77, 81, 82
8:23	81n13
8:28	11
9:8	24
10:2	121
10:17	109
11:16–24	111n54
12:2	14
16:20	6, 45

1 Corinthians

2:16	13
3:1–4	86
8:1	50
10:1–2	21n6
12:27	60
15:5–7	85
15:8	51n9, 85
15:20	76
15:45	87
15:47	87

2 Corinthians

1:6	70
4:10	68, 69
4:16	48n2
5:17	63, 92
5:19	92
11:2	59, 87
12:1–6	86
12:2–4	122

Galatians

1:16	107
2:19–20	71
2:20	68
3:14	110
3:16	6
3:21	102n37
4:4	15, 23
4:19	12, 59, 60, 67, 85, 93
5:7	123

Ephesians

1:3–14	6
1:22–23	58
2:19–22	49
2:22–23	50
4:11–13	86
4:12	50
4:13	48
4:15	50
4:16	50
5:25–32	23

Philippians

1:8	67
1:12–14	39
1:29	12
2:5–11	103
2:5	13, 69
2:9–11	41
2:11–12	15
3:8	12, 69
3:10	69, 70
3:11	70
3:20–21	87

Colossians

1:15	23, 56
1:18	37, 56
1:24	13, 70
1:27	57, 69
3:3	66

1 Thessalonians

1:10	87
5:2	87
5:3	57, 87

1 Timothy

2:5	8, 14, 40, 91
2:14–15	7n10
6:19	x

2 Timothy

1:10	38
2:8–10	12
3:1	57, 82

Hebrews

1:2	82
1:5	56
1:6	56
2:15	38
3:1–5	102n39
4:14	40
7:11	24
11:4	17
11:11	14
12:3	34
12:7–11	51
12:24	44

James

1:2–3	14
1:17	120

1 Peter

1:6–7	x, 14
1:23	24
2:5	50
3:17	11
3:19	11
4:13	14

2 Peter

3:4–5	74
3:5	80
3:6	80
3:7	79, 80
3:10	80
3:11–12	55
3:12	79
3:13	xiii, 82

1 John

3:2	66
4:8	4
4:9	23

Jude

20	50

Revelation

5:1	78
6:1–2	78
6:3–4	78
6:5–6	78
6:7	78
6:8	78
6:9–11	78
6:12–14	79
7:3	79
7:14	57, 78, 79
8:1	79
8:3	79
8:5	79
12:1–6	44, 55
12:1–2	18, 26
12:5	18, 26, 27
14:13	65, 76, 85
19:7–8	87
19:7	89, 93n2
19:8	48
20:13	76
21:1	73, 89
21:2	48, 51, 55, 59, 87, 93n2

Revelation *(continued)*

21:4	51
21:10	84
22:7	59
22:12	59
22:17	59, 87
22:20	59

Sirach

40:1	62, 76

4 Esdras

8:8	64

1 Enoch

47	70

www.ingramcontent.com/pod-product-compliance
Lightning Source LLC
Chambersburg PA
CBHW072145160426
43197CB00012B/2257